QUICK & EASY THAI

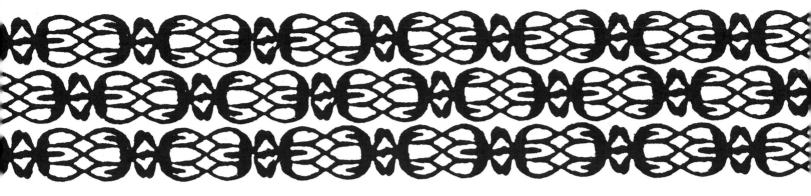

QUICK & EASY THAI

70 EVERYDAY RECIPES

by NANCIE McDERMOTT

photographs by ALISON MIKSCH

CHRONICLE BOOKS

SAN FRANCISCO

To my father, my inspiration in seeing the beauty of light and guiding me
toward my love of photography. —Alison Miksch

Text copyright © 2004 by Nancie McDermott.
Photographs copyright © 2004 by Alison Miksch.

Library of Congress Cataloging-in-Publication Data:

McDermott, Nancie.
Quick & easy Thai cooking : 70 everyday recipes / by Nancie McDermott.
photographs by Alison Miksch.
p. cm.
ISBN 978-0-8118-3731-6
1. Cookery, Thai. 2. Quick and easy cookery. I. Title: Quick and
easy Thai cooking. II. Miksch, Alison. III. Title.
TX724.5.T5M33 2004
641.5'55'09593—dc21
2003008935

Manufactured in China.

Designed by Lisa Billard Design, NY
Prop styling by Barbara Fritz
Food styling by William Smith

10 9

Chronicle Books LLC
680 Second Street
San Francisco, California 94107

www.chroniclebooks.com

This book is for my sweet sisters,

LINDA LLOYD McDERMOTT AND SUSANNE McDERMOTT SETTLE,

who are quick to laugh and easy to love.

TABLE *of* CONTENTS

INTRODUCTION

My goal in this book is to celebrate the extraordinary, delicious food of Thailand, and to help you cook Thai food at home with pleasure and success. To me, that means being able to put terrific, delicious Thai dishes on my table without devoting a weekend to the preparation and execution of a meal.

I first encountered Thai food as a Peace Corps volunteer, during the three years I spent teaching English as a second language in Thailand. In cafés and market stalls, bus stations, Buddhist temples, and in the homes of students and friends, I reveled in the chance to savor Thai food all day, every day. I devoured rice with countless delectable curries; I snacked on crisp golden fritters made with bananas, corn, or shrimp; I nibbled delectable chicken grilled on bamboo skewers; and I slurped away at steaming bowls of rice noodles in garlicky broth. Homesick for Thai food once I had returned to North Carolina, I began learning how to cook it in my Western kitchen.

Ingredients and equipment were difficult to find at that time, but to me the challenge was a plus. All week I taught school, but Saturdays I gladly spent tracking down a source for this coconut grater or that aromatic herb, standing beside Southeast Asian friends and watching them cook, and making Thai feasts in my tiny apartment kitchen for my family and friends. Newly married a few years later, I moved to Southern California, already home to enough people from Thailand, Laos, Cambodia, and Vietnam to support supermarkets filled with Asian food and tools. From fresh Thai chilies and wild lime leaves to sticky rice steamers and roasted chili paste, I suddenly had the vibrant world of Asian food close at hand. Soon I was teaching Thai cooking classes around the country, creating recipes and stories on Thai food for newspapers and magazines, and writing two of my previous cookbooks, *Real Thai: The Best of Thailand's Regional Cooking* (Chronicle Books, 1992) and *Real Vegetarian Thai* (Chronicle Books, 1997).

The great blessing of our two daughters meant the dawn of a new era in my kitchen, one in which I reacquainted myself with old friends like creamed corn, tomato soup, cottage cheese with pineapple, and cinnamon toast. I began to understand the despair I had seen on some of my students' faces as I presented a recipe with 23 ingredients and 19 steps. I gravitated toward dishes I could cook with one hand while the other hand held a telephone, a Raffi cassette, or a cookie. I found myself very interested in what I could do with the ten thousand items already awaiting me in my nearest grocery store, and far less attracted to the glorious and perfect ingredients available anywhere off my standard errand path.

I still love seeking out obscure traditional cooking utensils and reading up on the culinary legacy of the *Sukothai* period, and I am glad I took the time to master such street-food classics as crispy spring rolls and curry puffs, and such complex palace-style creations as *mee grop* and red curry seafood mousse steamed in banana-leaf cups. The results were magnificent, but required much from me: devotion to the task, considerable effort, quantities of time, and lots of shopping and dishes. I chose to undertake these projects, and I loved the process and the results, but quick and easy they were not.

Both girls are now in school and they not only adore red curry, our older daughter, Camellia, can make it for us. I still cook almost every night, and I still love to do it, but these days I want to balance my passion for cooking with my busy life. That life is bubbling along, overflowing with my wonderful children, my sweet husband, a little garden, a big dog, a faith community, helping out at school, going to the gym, walking with my neighbor, and keeping up with precious sisters, parents, and friends.

I wrote this book because I want to enjoy the dazzling flavors of Thai food even on a weeknight, to be able to cook Thai dishes as easily and happily and quickly as I make other favorite dishes for our table. To accomplish this, I focused on the enormous repertoire of Thai dishes that are intrinsically easy, the everyday food that Thai people cook at home. I also worked out recipes for great street food and classic restaurant dishes that are manageable in a home kitchen: most people in Thailand do not cook them, since they can stroll down to the night market for a bowl of noodles, a single serving of chicken with basil over rice, or a tall frosty glass of Thai iced tea. I also included a few dishes that would take too much time and effort in their pure form, for which I found reasonable shortcuts to a simpler but still wonderful version.

The result is this handbook to Thai cooking, filled with dishes that can become part of your everyday kitchen repertoire. A delectable spicy curry; a tureen of fragrant, nourishing soup; a plate of shrimp and snow peas with garlic and pepper; a pot of jasmine rice; a five-alarm salad of grilled beef seasoned so perfectly with chilies, lime juice, sugar, and fresh mint that it nearly puts out sparks: these are Thai dishes you can make anytime, anywhere, quickly and easily.

To give you background information about particular ingredients used in Thai cooking, I have included "A Thai Pantry" (page 154), along with "Mail-Order

Sources for Thai Ingredients" (page 162), to help you track down any items unavailable near your home. I have also provided you with detailed explanations of "Useful Utensils for Cooking Thai Food" (page 146) and "Techniques" (page 150), along with a list of "Menus for Quick & Easy Thai Meals" (page 142), to help you enjoy these recipes.

I hope this book will live in your kitchen, earning the stains and creases of frequent countertop use. I hope you will enjoy the Thai food you make, and the time you spend making it. I hope that you will cook often, and with friends, the way Thai people do, feeding themselves wonderfully, body and soul.

appetizers & snacks

INTRODUCTION TO APPETIZERS & SNACKS

This chapter sparkles with an array of contrasting dishes that epitomize the Thai philosophy of food; they're playful and varied, delicious and diverting, full of energy, surprises, and wit. Bright flavors abound, from brash chili sauces and tangy dressings to an aromatic breeze of lime juice, cilantro, and mint. This food makes noise, from the crunch of pork rinds and tart green apples to the sizzle of frying fish cakes and the hiss of satays browning over glowing coals. Garlicky spareribs invite you to lick your fingers, serene soft spring rolls look almost too pretty to eat, a bowl of Swedish meatballs turns out to be *panaeng* meatballs, in a luscious red curry sauce that definitely speaks Thai.

These dishes can be starters and snacks, in-between food for toting to potlucks or for getting people talking at your next open house. Some work with rice or noodles as part of a meal, and leftovers are always a treat. Cook Spicy Fish Cakes with Green Beans and Wild Lime Leaves (page 15) tonight, and make tomorrow's lunch a leftover fish cake on an onion roll, with lettuce and tomato and a dollop of mayonnaise spiked with red curry paste. Toss leftover satay sauce with spaghetti or macaroni, and enjoy with cucumber slices and spicy salsa on the side. Pick a recipe, shop a little, and start cooking. You will love the sparkling flavors, and you will be amazed how quickly and easily you can cook this food.

meatballs in panaeng curry sauce
panaeng look chin neua sahp

1½ cups unsweetened coconut milk

1 pound ground beef

½ teaspoon salt

2 tablespoons *panaeng* curry paste or red curry paste

½ cup water

1 tablespoon fish sauce

1 tablespoon palm sugar or brown sugar

6 wild lime leaves (optional)

This is my favorite contribution when we're invited to a party for which guests bring along something to share. Whether it's a Southern California potluck or a North Carolina covered-dish supper, my Thai version of meatballs disappears fast. My family loves it as a weeknight curry, along with Spinach with Black Pepper and Garlic (page 123), Easy Omelet with Sri Rachaa Sauce (page 59), and Jasmine Rice (page 100); or spooned over a bowl of noodles. If you don't have wild lime leaves, just substitute fresh basil or fresh cilantro, or omit the herbs altogether—it will still be delicious.

✿ Heat the coconut milk in a medium saucepan over medium heat, stirring occasionally, until it thickens a little and becomes smooth and fragrant, about 5 minutes.

✿ Meanwhile, season the ground beef with the salt and shape it into meatballs. Use about 1 tablespoon for each one, and place them on a plate.

✿ Add the curry paste to the saucepan and cook about 3 minutes more, mashing and stirring to dissolve the paste into the coconut milk. Add the meatballs and cook, turning gently to coat, 1 to 2 minutes.

✿ Increase the heat to medium-high, bring to a gentle boil, and add the water, fish sauce, and palm sugar. Crush the lime leaves, if using, in your hand and stir them in. Simmer, stirring gently now and then, until the meatballs are cooked through and the sauce is smooth, about 5 minutes. Remove from heat, transfer to a serving bowl, and serve hot or warm.

Makes 2 to 3 dozen meatballs

spicy fish cakes with green beans and wild lime leaves
tode mun plah

1 pound firm fish fillets, such as tilapia, catfish, rockfish, snapper, black bass, or salmon

1 egg

2 tablespoons red curry paste

1 tablespoon fish sauce

½ teaspoon sugar

½ teaspoon salt

3 to 4 raw green beans, very thinly sliced crosswise (about ¼ cup), or 2 green onions, very thinly sliced crosswise

8 wild lime leaves, very thinly sliced crosswise or minced

3 tablespoons vegetable oil

Tangy Cucumber Pickles (page 128)

This is a quintessentially Thai dish, traditionally consisting of very small, very chewy patties, deep-fried to a dark reddish brown. I like them that way but I also love them like this, plump and tender and easy to cook. You can make them without a food processor by simply cutting the fish into big chunks and then chopping these down to smaller pieces. You can prepare the seasoned fish mixture ahead of time and refrigerate, covered, for a day. Make it even without the lime leaves; it's still lovely.

⊛ Cut the fish fillets into big chunks, and then pulse them to a coarse paste in a food processor, stopping often to scrape the bowl, grinding the fish coarsely but fairly evenly without reducing it to a smooth paste. To use a blender, pulse the fish to a coarse paste in 3 or 4 batches, stopping often to scrape down the sides. Transfer the fish to a medium bowl and add the egg, curry paste, fish sauce, sugar, salt, green beans, and lime leaves. Use your hands to combine everything well. Shape into plump cakes, 2 to 3 inches in diameter, and set aside.

⊛ Heat the oil in a large, deep skillet or wok over medium-high heat until a bit of the fish mixture sizzles at once. Add half the cakes to the oil and fry for 3 to 5 minutes, until golden brown and cooked through, turning once. Drain well on paper towels, and then repeat with remaining cakes. Serve hot or warm with Tangy Cucumber Pickles.

Makes about 4 large or 8 small cakes

soft spring rolls with shrimp and fresh mint
miang yuan

8 ounces very thin dried rice noodles

12 round rice paper sheets, about 8 inches in diameter

10 leaves of bibb, Boston, or other tender lettuce, cut crosswise into 1-inch strips (about 2 cups loosely packed)

½ cup fresh mint leaves

½ cup fresh cilantro leaves

5 green onions, cut in 3-inch lengths and chopped lengthwise into thin strips

12 medium shrimp, cooked, peeled, and halved lengthwise

I enjoyed these delicate and delightful snacks in Vietnamese cafes in the north-eastern Thai metropolis of Ubon Rachatahnii, which, like most larger towns in the vicinity of the Mekong river, has a sizable Vietnamese community. Soft spring rolls are a pleasure to see and to eat, and simple to make if you set up a small assembly line with all the components ready to roll up. The secret Thai ingredient here is extra pairs of hands, to make the job sa-nuk: light-hearted, happy, interesting, and fun. Recruit some helpers and make a double or triple batch. You can hold them for several hours at room temperature, loosely covered with a damp kitchen towel or a sheet of plastic wrap. Serve with Sweet-Hot Garlic Sauce (page 129) or prik nahm plah, a small bowl of fish sauce topped with minced fresh hot green chilies.

✸ Bring a medium saucepan of water to a rolling boil over high heat. Drop in the rice noodles, and remove from the heat. Let stand 8 to 10 minutes, gently lifting and stirring the noodles now and then as they soften, to keep them separate and to cook evenly. Drain, rinse with cold water, drain well, and set aside. You should have about 2 cups of noodles.

✸ Arrange all the ingredients separately around a large cutting board or tray set before you. Set out a platter to hold the finished rolls, as well as a large skillet or shallow bowl filled with very warm water.

✸ To make each roll, slide 1 sheet of rice paper into the pan of water and press gently to submerge it for about 15 seconds. Remove it carefully, draining the water, and place it before you on the cutting board.

continued

❁ Line up a horizontal row of each of the following ingredients on the rice paper sheet, starting on the lowest third of the sheet and working away from you: a small tangle of noodles (about ¼ cup), a row of lettuce strips, a row of mint leaves, a row of cilantro leaves, and a row of green onion slivers on top.

❁ Lift the wrapper edge nearest to you and roll it away from you, up and over the fillings, tucking it in under them about halfway along the wrapper and compressing everything gently into a cylinder shape. When you've completely enclosed the filling in one good turn, fold in the right and left sides tightly, as though making an envelope. Then place 2 shrimp halves, pink-side down, on the rice sheet just above the cylinder. Continue rolling up the wrapper and press the seam to close it, wetting it with a little splash of water if it has dried out too much to seal itself closed. Set the roll aside on the platter to dry, seam-side down. Continue to fill and roll up the rice paper sheets with the remaining ingredients until you have made 8 to 10 rolls. Set aside.

❁ To serve, present the rolls whole, or halved crosswise, straight or on the diagonal, or trim away ends and cut into bite-sized lengths.

Makes 8 to 10 rolls

spicy cashew salad with chilies, cilantro, and lime
yum meht mahmuang himapahn

Vegetable oil for frying

1 cup fresh raw whole cashews
 (about ¼ pound)

½ teapoon salt

3 tablespoons coarsely chopped shallots

3 tablespoons thinly sliced green onions

2 teaspoons dried red chili flakes

2 tablespoons freshly squeezed lime juice

You may think that cashews are nearly perfect already, but try this simple preparation and you will agree with me that sometimes a good thing can get even better. Raw cashews are widely available in Asian markets at a reasonable price, and they keep a long time uncooked. You can add a big spoonful of dried shrimp, if you like them, and offer a plate of small lettuce cups so your guests can scoop up these delectable cashews bite by bite.

❀ Line a plate with a double layer of paper towels, and place it by the stove, along with a slotted spoon or an Asian-style wire-mesh strainer. Heat 2 or 3 inches of vegetable oil in a medium skillet or wok over medium heat until a raw cashew begins to sizzle a few seconds after you add it to the oil, 4 to 5 minutes. Keep one raw cashew handy by the stove to help you judge the changes in color as the nuts cook.

❀ Gently add cashews and cook, stirring gently and often, until the nuts turn a soft, pale golden brown, 2 to 3 minutes. Scoop the cashews out onto the prepared plate, using a slotted spoon or a wire-mesh strainer. Let them drain and cool a little while you set out a medium bowl and a small serving platter.

❀ Turn the still-warm cashews into the bowl and toss with the salt. Add the shallots, green onions, and chili flakes and toss well. Just before serving, add the lime juice, toss well, and mound on the serving platter. Serve warm or at room temperature, with small spoons for eating, or as finger food.

Serves 3 to 4

thai crab cakes
boo jah

1 tablespoon chopped garlic

1 tablespoon chopped fresh cilantro roots, or stems and leaves, plus a handful of fresh cilantro leaves, coarsely chopped

2 tablespoons water

1 tablespoon fish sauce

1 teaspoon soy sauce

½ teaspoon salt

½ teaspoon freshly ground pepper

¾ pound cooked lump crabmeat

½ pound ground pork

½ cup bread crumbs or mashed potatoes

1 egg, beaten

All-purpose flour for dredging

2 tablespoons vegetable oil

Seaside cafes all along the Gulf of Siam make hearty, delicious crab cakes with pork, garlic, and pepper. Fresh crabmeat is spectacular in this dish, but canned also works fine. In the classic Thai presentation, the mixture is stuffed into crab shells, steamed, and then fried, filling-side down, until golden and crisp. This version is just as delicious, but much quicker to make. Serve with a simple spicy sauce, such as Sri Rachaa sauce, Sweet-Hot Garlic Sauce (page 129), or mayonnaise spiked with either roasted chili paste (nahm prik pao) *or red curry paste and chopped green onions.*

❀ In a small food processor or blender jar, combine the garlic, cilantro roots, water, fish sauce, soy sauce, salt, and pepper and blend well until fairly smooth. In a medium bowl, combine the garlic-cilantro mixture with the crabmeat, pork, bread crumbs, cilantro leaves, and egg and mix gently. Shape the crabmeat mixture into 8 plump cakes, each about 3 inches in diameter. Put the flour on a dinner plate, dip each crab cake in the flour to coat it lightly, and place it on a platter by the stove.

❀ Heat the oil in a large skillet over medium-high heat for about 1 minute, until a pinch of flour sizzles at once. Add 4 cakes to the oil and fry, turning once, until golden brown and cooked through, 5 to 7 minutes. Drain well on paper towels, and then repeat with remaining cakes. Transfer the cakes to a serving platter and serve hot or warm.

Makes about 8 crab cakes

northern-style dipping sauce with ground pork and tomatoes
nahm prik ohng

3 tablespoons vegetable oil

2 tablespoons finely chopped garlic

2 tablespoons chopped shallots

1 tablespoon red curry paste

½ pound ground pork

20 cherry tomatoes or 5 roma (plum)
  tomatoes, coarsely chopped

½ cup water

3 tablespoons fish sauce

1 tablespoon brown sugar

Optional Accompaniments

Cucumbers, peeled and sliced into thick
  ovals (about 1½ cups)

Green beans, trimmed to 2-inch lengths
  (about 1½ cups)

2 wedges cabbage, about 2 inches across at
  widest part

Sticky Rice (page 98)

Crisp-fried pork rinds

The classic Northern Thai khan toke *meal includes this hearty dish, a specialty of the Tai Yai, or Shan, people. It is a winner, with easy-to-find ingredients, straightforward methods, and terrific flavor. I love it with sticky rice and* kaeb moo, *crunchy pork rinds that are easy to find here in North Carolina. Traditionally,* nahm prik ohng *is served in a small bowl along with sticky rice and an array of crisp, raw vegetables for dipping in and scooping up the chunky sauce. My family enjoys it without them as well, paired with Jasmine Rice (page 100) and a big green salad for a speedy and satisfying weeknight supper. If I have any leftover* nahm prik ohng, *I toss it with noodles and cucumber slices for a quick lunch.*

❈   In a medium skillet or wok, heat the oil over medium heat and then add the garlic and shallots. Cook, tossing now and then, 1 to 2 minutes, until they are shiny and fragrant. Add the curry paste and cook, mashing and stirring well to soften, about 1 minute longer.

❈   Add the pork and toss well. Stir in the tomatoes, water, fish sauce, and brown sugar, and bring to a gentle boil. Cook 5 to 7 minutes, stirring now and then. Remove from heat and transfer to a small serving bowl. Serve warm or at room temperature, with one or more of the optional accompaniments, or with rice.

Serves 4 to 6

crispy pork spareribs with black pepper and garlic
gradook moo tote

2 tablespoons coarsely chopped garlic

2 tablespoons coarsely chopped fresh cilantro roots, or stems and leaves, plus a handful of fresh cilantro leaves

1 teaspoon freshly ground pepper

2 or 3 tablespoons water

3 tablespoons fish sauce

1 teaspoon sugar

2 pounds pork spareribs

Vegetable oil for deep-frying

For the bite-sized spareribs traditional in Thailand, ask the butcher to cut a rack of pork spareribs across the bone into 1-inch lengths. Then cut lengthwise between the bones to separate the ribs into meaty pieces. Or, leave the ribs whole and oven-roast or grill. These are great: your guests will be licking their fingers.

❀ Grind the garlic, cilantro roots, pepper, and water into a fairly smooth paste, using a small food processor or a blender (or use a fork to mash them on your cutting board along with the sugar). Scrape the seasoning paste into a medium bowl and stir in the fish sauce and sugar. Add the ribs and toss to coat well. Cover the bowl and refrigerate for 30 minutes to 1 hour.

❀ Add about 3 inches of vegetable oil to a deep-frying pan or a wok. Over medium heat, bring the oil to frying temperature, 350 to 375 degrees F. Meanwhile, set a plate lined with paper towels or a brown paper bag by the stove, for draining the cooked ribs. Also set out a long-handled wire-mesh scoop or a slotted spoon for transferring the cooked ribs to the plate.

❀ When the oil is hot enough to make a bit of garlic sizzle at once, add about a third of the ribs. Gently separate them as they sizzle and foam in the oil. Fry, turning them occasionally, until they are evenly browned and cooked through, 4 to 6 minutes. Scoop the ribs out and place them in a single layer on the prepared plate. Cook the remaining two batches the same way.

❀ Pile the ribs on a serving platter, garnish with a small bouquet of cilantro leaves on the side, and serve warm, along with a bowl for the leftover bones.

Serves 4 to 6

chicken satay with spicy peanut sauce
gai satay

Marinade for Chicken

½ cup unsweetened coconut milk

1 teaspoon fish sauce

1 teaspoon brown sugar

1 teaspoon curry powder

1 pound boneless, skinless chicken thighs
  or breasts

Spicy Peanut Sauce

¾ cup unsweetened coconut milk

1 tablespoon red curry paste, or
  mussamun curry paste

2 teaspoons roasted chili paste
  (*nahm prik pao*; optional)

½ cup chicken broth or water

1 tablespoon fish sauce

1 tablespoon palm sugar or brown sugar

¼ cup chunky peanut butter or very finely
  ground peanuts

1 tablespoon freshly squeezed lime juice or
  tamarind liquid (see page 150)

About 60 bamboo skewers, soaked in water
  for at least 30 minutes

Tangy Cucumber Pickles (page 128)

This dish looks inviting, tastes fantastic, and is fun to eat. To make in advance, marinate the meat, put the cucumber pickles together, make the sauce, and then cover and chill. Let your first guests skewer the meat and get it grilling while you gently reheat the peanut sauce. This way you will have time to make a quick batch of the traditional satay accompaniment: toast! Thais often serve satay with a side of toast points, the better to enjoy the fabulous peanut sauce.

❀ Combine the coconut milk, fish sauce, brown sugar, and curry powder in a large mixing bowl and stir well. Cut chicken thighs into generous, bite-sized chunks, and cut breast meat lengthwise into ½-inch strips. Add the meat to the marinade and mix well. Cover and refrigerate for at least 30 minutes or as long as overnight.

❀ To prepare the peanut sauce, bring the coconut milk to a gentle boil in a medium saucepan over medium-high heat. Add the curry paste and roasted chili paste and cook 4 to 5 minutes, mashing and stirring occasionally to dissolve them. Add the chicken broth, fish sauce, palm sugar, peanut butter, and lime juice and cook 1 minute more, stirring well to make a smooth sauce. Remove from heat, transfer to a small serving bowl, and set aside to cool. The sauce can be served warm or at room temperature, or cover and refrigerate, reheating gently just before serving time.

❀ Thread meat onto tips of bamboo skewers, and cook on a lightly oiled, hot grill or under a broiler, turning often, until browned and cooked through, 4 to 6 minutes. Serve at once with the peanut sauce and Tangy Cucumber Pickles.

Serves 6 to 8

soups

INTRODUCTION TO SOUPS

Thai soups must be the easiest of all these quick and easy Thai dishes to prepare. Most of the work happens on the stove during a simmering session, not even a very long one when compared to soup-making in the West. Once you have cut up some meat, sliced a few green onions, or whacked a stalk of lemongrass to release its perfume, you assemble the players in a pot and leave them to it. You are free to read, or peel a mango, or refill the sugar bowl, but do not pick up the telephone or try to nap; you will not have time. Most Thai soups come together so fast that you will want to put the rice on first, and leave any additions of lime juice or scattering of cilantro and green onion for the last minute. Those aromatic touches should come right before serving, when the soup is steaming hot.

A word about Thai soups and rice. Rice is the essence of the Thai meal, and Thai soups evolved as intensely seasoned partners to it. Soups in the West stand alone, either as a first course or as a simple meal with salad and bread. Thai soups join other dishes to compose a rice meal, each playing off the other with its contrasting flavor. For hot, spicy notes Thais might choose the Shrimp and Lemongrass Soup (page 30); for voluptuous, tangy notes, the Chicken-Coconut Soup (page 28); and for smooth, salty notes, the Meatball Soup with Spinach and Crispy Garlic (page 29).

But you, dear reader, are not to worry about strictly following the Rules for Soup. You are expected only to pick a soup, put it together, start it simmering, and then enjoy it when it is ready. You may serve the soup alone as a first course, or offer it Thai style with rice and other dishes. You may even build a little meal around it, savoring it with a baked potato, polenta, or bread. Perhaps some pasta, a green salad, or buttery corn on the cob? As they say in Thailand, *dtahm jai;* "suit yourself."

chicken-coconut soup
tome kah gai

2 tablespoons freshly squeezed lime juice

2 tablespoons fish sauce

2 green onions, very thinly sliced crosswise

6 wild lime leaves, torn or cut in quarters
  (optional)

2 tablespoons coarsely chopped fresh cilantro

1½ cups unsweetened coconut milk

1½ cups chicken broth or water

10 to 12 slices galanga, fresh, frozen, or dried

2 stalks fresh lemongrass

¾ pound boneless chicken, cut into big,
  bite-sized chunks

1 cup thinly sliced fresh mushrooms

Back in North Carolina after my Peace Corps service, and homesick for Thailand, I tried making this soup. To my amazement, it was spectacular, bright and bracing with lime juice and galanga, and comforting, like all the world's chicken soups. It was so easy and so good, it inspired me to keep right on cooking Thai food. I used big woody chips of dried galanga for my first version of this soup; thin, crisp slices of fresh galanga after I moved out to Southern California; and fresh ginger, galanga's first cousin, whenever I ran out of either one. They all made an extraordinary tome kah gai, *or in the case of the fresh ginger version,* tome king gai. *Now that I am back in North Carolina, I use slices of frozen galanga imported from Thailand. For family meals I leave the galanga and lemongrass in the soup, Thai style, but for company I strain them out.*

❀ In a large serving bowl combine the lime juice, fish sauce, green onions, and half the wild lime leaves, if using. Place this bowl by the stove, along with a small bowl containing the chopped cilantro.

❀ In a medium saucepan, combine the coconut milk and chicken broth and bring to a gentle boil over medium-high heat. Stir in the galanga, lemongrass, and remaining lime leaves. Add the chicken and mushrooms, return to a gentle boil, and simmer gently until chicken is cooked through, about 10 minutes.

❀ Remove from heat, pour the hot soup over the herbs and seasonings in the serving bowl, and stir well. Sprinkle with the chopped cilantro and serve hot.

Serves 4 to 6

meatball soup with spinach and crispy garlic
gaeng jeut look chin moo ru neua

4 cups water

3 tablespoons vegetable oil

2 tablespoons coarsely chopped garlic

½ pound ground pork or ground beef

About 8 cups fresh spinach leaves, washed and trimmed (about 10 ounces)

2 green onions, thinly sliced crosswise

1 tablespoon fish sauce

½ teaspoon salt

¼ teaspoon freshly ground pepper

Too busy or too tired to cook, but too hungry not to? This is the soup for you. Served Thai style, it goes with rice and other dishes, but if you ladle the soup over a big bowl of cooked rice noodles, jasmine rice, or elbow macaroni, you will have a one-pot, one-bowl, satisfying meal. I use a bag of washed, prepped spinach, preferably the sturdy, curly, dark green kind, but baby spinach leaves are also fine, as are Swiss chard, watercress, or bok choy.

❀ In a medium saucepan over medium-high heat, bring the water to a rolling boil. Meanwhile, for the crispy garlic in oil: Place a small heatproof bowl by the stove. Heat the oil in a small frying pan over medium heat until a bit of garlic sizzles at once. Add the garlic and cook, stirring often, until it is fragrant and golden, 1 to 2 minutes. Remove from heat, pour hot garlic and oil into the heatproof bowl, and set aside to cool.

❀ When the water is boiling wildly, add the ground pork in generous pinches, by hand or by teaspoons, making free-form meatballs. Stir well, and simmer 3 to 4 minutes until meat is cooked.

❀ Remove from heat and stir in the spinach, green onions, fish sauce, salt, and pepper. Transfer to a serving bowl, pour the crispy garlic and oil mixture over the soup, and serve hot.

Makes 4 servings

shrimp and lemongrass soup
tome yum goong

3 tablespoons freshly squeezed lime juice

1 tablespoon thinly sliced fresh hot
  green chilies

2 green onions, very thinly sliced crosswise

6 wild lime leaves, torn or cut in quarters
  (optional)

2 tablespoons coarsely chopped fresh
  cilantro leaves

3 cups water, chicken broth, or shrimp stock

3 stalks fresh lemongrass, trimmed to
  3-inch base and cut on the diagonal into
  1-inch lengths

5 slices galanga, fresh, frozen, or dried

½ pound medium shrimp, peeled
  and deveined

1 cup thinly sliced fresh mushrooms

2 tablespoons fish sauce

2 tablespoons roasted chili paste
  (*nahm prik pao*; optional)

Although world-renowned as the fiery queen of Thai soups, tome yum *is very much a quick and easy dish. You need the lemongrass, but you can still make a tasty* tome yum *without the galanga and wild lime leaves. The roasted chili paste fortifies the broth wonderfully, but it is not essential either. You can also make a rustic, northeastern Thai version of* tome yum *using chunks of catfish or salmon instead of shrimp, adding a generous handful of halved cherry tomatoes and a quintet of tiny Thai chilies, whole ones, stemmed and crushed lightly to release a little extra heat.*

❀ In a large serving bowl combine the lime juice, chilies, green onions, and half the lime leaves, if using. Place this bowl by the stove, along with a small bowl containing the chopped cilantro.

❀ In a medium saucepan, combine the water, lemongrass, galanga, and remaining lime leaves, if using. Bring to a boil over medium-high heat and cook for 3 to 4 minutes. Add the shrimp and mushrooms to the broth, and cook 2 to 3 minutes more, until the mushrooms are tender and the shrimp are cooked.

❀ Stir in the fish sauce and roasted chili paste, if using, and remove from heat. Pour the hot soup over the lime juice and herbs in the serving bowl, and stir well. Sprinkle with the chopped cilantro and serve hot.

Serves 4 to 6

catfish soup with bamboo shoots
gaeng leuang plah

3 cups water

3 tablespoons *gaeng leuan*g curry paste, or
   3 tablespoons red curry paste plus
   2 teaspoons curry powder

15 fresh green beans, trimmed and
   halved crosswise

1 cup drained sliced canned bamboo shoots

1 cup thin, bite-sized chunks fresh pineapple
   or drained, canned pineapple chunks

1 pound meaty white fish fillets, such as
   tilapia, catfish, snapper, grouper, or cod, cut
   crosswise into 2-inch chunks

2 tablespoons fish sauce

2 tablespoons tamarind liquid (see page 150),
   Indian-style tamarind chutney, or freshly
   squeezed lime juice

1 tablespoon palm sugar or brown sugar

1 tablespoon freshly squeezed lime juice

This signature dish of Thailand's lush southern region is terrific with Spinach with Black Pepper and Garlic (page 123) and a steaming bowl of Jasmine Rice (page 100). Delicious and pretty, this soup has lots of ingredients, but all you do is a little chopping and a bit of stirring.

❀   In a medium saucepan, bring the water to a gentle boil over medium heat, and then stir in the curry paste, green beans, bamboo shoots, and pineapple. Stir well and simmer 5 minutes.

❀   Add the fish chunks, fish sauce, tamarind liquid, and palm sugar, and cook 3 to 5 minutes, until fish is cooked through. Remove from heat and transfer to a serving bowl. Stir in the lime juice, and serve hot.

Serves 4 to 6

rice soup with chicken, cilantro, and crispy garlic
kao tome gai

3 tablespoons vegetable oil

2 tablespoons coarsely chopped garlic

4 cups chicken stock

2 cups cooked rice

¼ pound ground pork, chicken, or turkey

1 tablespoon fish sauce

1 teaspoon freshly ground pepper

1 tablespoon minced fresh ginger (optional)

3 green onions, thinly sliced crosswise

A handful of fresh cilantro leaves, coarsely chopped

Simply delicious and simple to make, this is Thai-style comfort food. Thais eat kao tome *for breakfast, supper, or as a midnight meal at a cafe after a night on the town. It's the first choice when Thais cook for someone who's under the weather, but I make it whenever we need a quick and hearty one-dish supper that satisfies us all. In Thailand, coarsely ground pork is most popular, but other meats work well, including ground turkey or chicken, leftover roast duck, or roast chicken. Shrimp is also divine, but take care to remove the soup from the heat as soon as it is cooked through.*

❀ Place a small heatproof bowl by the stove. Heat the oil in a small frying pan over medium heat until a bit of garlic sizzles at once. Add the garlic and cook, stirring often, until it is fragrant and golden, 1 to 2 minutes. Remove from heat, pour hot garlic and oil into the heatproof bowl, and set aside to cool.

❀ Bring the chicken stock to a boil in a medium saucepan over medium-high heat, and then stir in the cooked rice. When the soup returns to a boil, add the ground pork in generous pinches, by hand or by teaspoons, making free-form meatballs. Stir well, and add the fish sauce. Simmer 3 to 4 minutes, until meat is cooked.

❀ Transfer the hot soup to a serving bowl and top with the crispy garlic in oil, pepper, ginger (if using), green onions, and cilantro. Just before serving, stir well and serve hot.

Serves 4 to 6

tangy salmon soup with fresh ginger and tamarind
tome some plah

3 cups water

3 tablespoons coarsely chopped shallots

2 tablespoons coarsely chopped fresh cilantro roots, or stems and leaves, plus 2 tablespoons coarsely chopped fresh cilantro leaves

½ teaspoon freshly ground pepper

3-inch chunk of fresh ginger, peeled and shredded or finely chopped

¾ pound meaty fish fillets, such as salmon, catfish, or tilapia

¼ cup tamarind liquid (see page 150), Indian-style tamarind chutney, or freshly squeezed lime juice

2 tablespoons fish sauce

2 tablespoons palm sugar or brown sugar

½ teaspoon salt

2 tablespoons thinly sliced green onions

A beautiful soup, delicate and nourishing, with the flavor of Thai country life. Freshwater fish are typically used, but salmon is my favorite and shrimp make a marvelous special-occasion version. To cut fresh ginger into fine threads, peel and slice it crosswise into very thin coins, stack the coins in little piles, and cut into very thin strips. If this is too much work, just mince it up and toss it in.

❀ In a small food processor or a blender, combine ½ cup of the water with the shallots, cilantro roots, and pepper, and grind to a fairly smooth paste. (Or finely chop the shallots and cilantro roots and mix with the pepper to make a coarse paste.) In a medium saucepan, combine the shallot-cilantro paste with the ginger and the remaining 2½ cups water and bring to a boil over medium-high heat.

❀ Meanwhile, cut the fish in half lengthwise and cut each long section crosswise into 2-inch chunks. When the broth reaches a boil, reduce the heat to medium, add the fish, and let the soup return to a boil.

❀ Add the tamarind liquid, fish sauce, palm sugar, and salt and return soup to a boil. Remove from heat and transfer to a serving bowl. Stir in the green onions and cilantro leaves, and serve hot.

Serves 4

curries

INTRODUCTION TO CURRIES

Curries are at the heart of Thailand's extraordinary cuisine. Thai curry pastes, the key to these unique, satisfying dishes, begin with a foundation of shallots, garlic, and cilantro root, ground down to a fragrant mush. Fresh lemongrass, pungent ivory slices of galanga, and a flourish of wild lime peel bring a dazzling herbal element to the mixture. Spice notes come from cumin and coriander seeds, roasted to deepen their flavor. Little explosions of heat come from wildly hot fresh green chilies or fiercely hot dried red ones, and from peppercorns, native to Southeast Asia and the original source of fiery Thai flavors. All this excitement could take one right over the edge, but not in the deft hands of Thai cooks.

Thai curries invite you on a little excursion, one you are destined to remember with pleasure at journey's end. Off you go, weaving through traffic, darting down one alley and up another, slipping into an opening that materializes unexpectedly. The driver of this imaginary taxi is playful but highly skilled, mindful of the destination and determined to get you there happy, albeit a bit dazed the first few times you make the trip. Coconut milk softens the heat. Fresh basil and wild lime leaves awaken the senses. Winter squash, potatoes, and pineapple add substance, and rice or rice noodles make you take your time eating. You are happy and you want a little more.

With all that grinding of all those special ingredients, you may wonder whether Thai curries have a place in this quick and easy book. They certainly do, thanks to the fact that Thai curry pastes are widely available these days, in supermarkets and specialty food shops as well as in Asian markets. With prepared curry paste in one hand and unsweetened coconut milk in the other, you are about fifteen

minutes away from a fantastic meal, alive with the complex, diverting flavors of Thai cuisine.

Each recipe calls for a specific kind of curry paste, but rest assured you can substitute any Thai curry paste for another in these recipes, and vary the other ingredients as well. Once you can make Red Curry Beef with Butternut Squash (page 47), or Green Curry Chicken with Zucchini (page 40), you can make green curry with chicken and asparagus, or *mussamun* curry with lamb, yams, and cashews. Red Curry Shrimp with Pineapple (page 48) leads you right on over to green curry with shrimp and sugar snap peas, or red curry with salmon and sweet red peppers. With a supply of coconut milk, curry paste, and fish sauce on your pantry shelf, you will be ready to mix and match what you have on hand and create a curry using the ingredients you like best.

Start the rice or pasta pot before you make the curry: they will take just a bit longer to cook. But you could also warm a stack of tortillas when dinner is ready, or cook up a quick pot of couscous, or cut thick slices of good bread. You have lots of options, but I am sure you will want rice, noodles, or bread. Otherwise, how will you soak up every last drop of your delicious Thai curry sauce?

quick red curry paste
krueng gaeng peht

3 large dried red New Mexico or Anaheim chili peppers

10 small dried red chilies, such as *chiles de arbol* or *chiles japones*

½ cup coarsely chopped shallots or onions

¼ cup coarsely chopped garlic

1 tablespoon coarsely chopped fresh ginger or fresh or frozen galanga

1 tablespoon ground coriander

1 teaspoon ground cumin

½ teaspoon freshly ground pepper

½ teaspoon salt

This simple red curry paste is easy to make and fun to compare with the prepared Thai curry pastes on the market. Homemade curry pastes are generally beyond the scope of a quick and easy approach, but if you cannot find red curry paste or simply want to learn more about Thailand's curry traditions, here is a basic recipe. The chilies can soak while you prepare and measure out the remaining ingredients.

If you would like to simplify it even more, omit the ground coriander, cumin, and pepper, to make gaeng kua *curry paste. If you would like to further expand the recipe's flavor, add any or all of the following to the paste before you grind it: 2 tablespoons minced fresh lemongrass; 2 tablespoons chopped cilantro roots, or cilantro stems and leaves; or 4 finely chopped wild lime leaves.*

⚜ Stem and seed the large and small dried red chilies, break them in large pieces, and place them in a small bowl. Add warm water to cover and set aside while you prepare the remaining ingredients.

⚜ In the workbowl of a small food processor or a blender, combine the shallots, garlic, ginger, coriander, cumin, pepper, and salt. Add the softened chilies, along with ¼ cup of the soaking water. Process everything to a fairly smooth purée, stopping now and then to scrape down the sides, and add more soaking water, a tablespoon or two at a time, if you need it to help grinding. Transfer the paste to a small jar and cover tightly. The paste can be stored in the refrigerator for about 3 weeks, or in the freezer for about 3 months.

Makes about ¾ cup

green curry chicken with zucchini
gaeng kiow wahn gai

2 medium zucchini or 2 long purple
  Asian eggplants

1½ cups unsweetened coconut milk

2 to 3 tablespoons green curry paste

¾ pound boneless chicken thighs or breast,
  cut in big, bite-sized pieces

1½ cups chicken broth or water

2 tablespoons fish sauce

1 tablespoon palm sugar or brown sugar

6 to 8 wild lime leaves, torn or cut in half
  (optional)

A handful of fresh Asian or Italian basil leaves,
  plus basil sprigs for garnish

Green curry gets its name from the profusion of fresh hot green chilies fortifying the curry paste, rather than from the color of the finished curry. Some say it is the hottest of all Thai curries, but curry heat depends both upon how a given curry paste is made, and how much of it the cook stirs into the curry pot. The classic green curry uses chicken with lots of golfball-sized Thai eggplant, known as makeua poh, *along with a flourish of the tiny, fragrant eggplant called* makeua peuang, *which adds a unique herbal note to the curry. I like it with chicken thighs cut into generous chunks and zucchini or yellow squash, or some of both. Long purple Asian eggplant makes a fabulous alternative. The lime leaves and basil are lovely, but not essential to a great green curry.*

❀ Cut the zucchini in half lengthwise and then crosswise into 1-inch chunks; set aside. In a medium saucepan or heavy skillet, bring ¾ cup of the coconut milk to a gentle boil over medium-high heat. Cook for 2 to 3 minutes, until it begins to thicken and becomes fragrant. Add the curry paste and cook 2 to 3 minutes, pressing and stirring to dissolve it into the coconut milk. Add the chicken and cook 2 minutes more, tossing to coat it with the sauce.

❀ Add the remaining ¾ cup coconut milk, the chicken broth, zucchini, fish sauce, palm sugar, and about half the wild lime leaves, if using, and bring to a gentle boil. Reduce heat to maintain a lively simmer and cook, stirring now and then, until the chicken is cooked and the zucchini is tender but still firm, 8 to 10 minutes. Remove from the heat and stir in the remaining lime leaves and the fresh basil leaves. Garnish with a few sprigs of fresh basil and serve hot or warm.

Serves 4 to 6

yellow curry chicken with potatoes
gaeng kah-ree gai

2¾ cups unsweetened coconut milk

3 tablespoons yellow (*kah-ree*) curry paste, or 3 tablespoons red curry paste plus 1 tablespoon curry powder

6 boneless chicken thighs, cut into big, bite-sized chunks, or about 1 pound boneless chicken breast, sliced crosswise into 2-inch strips

2 cups chicken broth or water

2 medium potatoes, peeled and cut into big, bite-sized chunks (about 1½ cups)

1 medium onion, cut lengthwise into thick wedges (about 1 cup)

2 tablespoons fish sauce

1 tablespoon palm sugar or brown sugar

This sunny yellow curry practically cooks itself, and its pleasing flavor blossoms even more the day after it is made. It is terrific with shrimp as well as with chicken. Stir in the shrimp at the end when the potatoes are tender, and cook only until the shrimp turn pink and are cooked through. The classic accompaniment for gaeng kah-ree *and rice is Tangy Cucumber Pickles (page 128), or a bowl of sliced cucumbers when time is short.*

❀   In a medium saucepan or heavy skillet, bring 1 cup of the coconut milk to a gentle boil over medium-high heat. Cook for 2 to 3 minutes, until it begins to thicken and becomes fragrant. Add the curry paste and cook 2 to 3 minutes, pressing and stirring to dissolve it into the coconut milk. Add the chicken and cook another minute or two, tossing to coat it with the sauce.

❀   Add the remaining 1¾ cups coconut milk, the chicken broth, potatoes, onion, fish sauce, and palm sugar, and bring to a boil. Reduce heat to maintain a lively simmer and cook, stirring now and then, until the chicken is cooked and the potatoes are tender but still firm, 6 to 8 minutes. Remove from the heat and serve hot or warm.

Serves 6 to 8

braised chicken in yellow curry
gai goh-lae

2 tablespoons vegetable oil

2 pounds chicken thighs or any combination of chicken pieces

3 tablespoons yellow curry paste, or 3 tablespoons red curry paste plus 1 tablespoon curry powder

1½ cups unsweetened coconut milk

2½ cups chicken broth

2 tablespoons fish sauce

2 tablespoons freshly squeezed lime juice, or 2 tablespoons white vinegar plus 2 teaspoons sugar

1 tablespoon palm sugar or brown sugar

This tasty curry from southern Thailand shows its Malay roots in its use of whole, bone-in chicken pieces, first browned and then braised in a spice-infused curry sauce to aromatic perfection. The word goh-lae *means the traditional wooden fishing boats still plying the warm waters of the Gulf of Siam, their hulls painted in spectacular, multicolored designs. If you have time for an extra step, combine a teaspoon each of ground cumin, coriander, cinnamon, and curry powder in a small skillet. Toast them for a minute or two over medium heat until fragrant and lightly browned, and add along with the curry paste mixture. You can use fried, roasted, or grilled chicken pieces here, adding them along with the coconut milk after you've cooked the curry paste. For chicken breasts, I like to cut each one into 2 or 3 pieces before using in this recipe.*

❀ In a 3-quart saucepan, heat the vegetable oil over medium-high heat. Brown the chicken pieces in two batches, turning once or twice until golden and then transferring the browned pieces to a medium bowl.

❀ Reduce heat to medium and add the curry paste to the saucepan. Cook, stirring and mashing, until the paste is fragrant and softened, about 2 minutes. Return the chicken and its juices to the pan and add the coconut milk and chicken broth. Bring to a gentle boil, adjust heat to maintain a lively simmer, and cook 15 to 20 minutes, until chicken is tender and cooked through. Stir in the fish sauce, lime juice, and palm sugar and remove from heat. Transfer to a serving bowl and serve hot or warm.

Serves 6 to 8

mussamun curry beef with potatoes and peanuts
gaeng mussamun neua

1 pound boneless beef, such as tri-tip, flank steak, or rib eye; or 1 pound boneless chicken thighs or breast; or 8 chicken legs

3 cups unsweetened coconut milk

¼ cup *mussamun* curry paste

2½ cups chicken or beef broth

3 medium potatoes, peeled and cut in big, bite-sized chunks (about 2 cups)

1 large onion, quartered lengthwise and cut in large chunks (about 1½ cups)

3 tablespoons fish sauce

1 tablespoon palm sugar or brown sugar

1 teaspoon salt

1 cup dry-roasted salted peanuts

2 tablespoons freshly squeezed lime juice, or tamarind liquid (page 150), or Indian-style tamarind chutney

Vibrant with a chorus of cinnamon, nutmeg, mace, cloves, and cardamom, mussamun curry is the centerpiece of celebration meals throughout the Thai kingdom. In the classic version, generous chunks of beef are simmered slowly in coconut milk until tender, then seasoned with tamarind and infused with an elaborate paste redolent of sweet spices. Thais love it with chicken as well, especially drumsticks.

Here I have used tender beef sliced thinly to cook quickly. You can also use ground beef or lamb shaped into meatballs, or chicken legs or wings. Any way you make it, gaeng mussamun is a glorious dish, our house curry for parties, and for carrying to potluck suppers along with jasmine rice. Originating in the Muslim communities of southern Thailand, mussamun curry always makes a memorable feast.

❀ Slice beef crosswise into very thin, 2-inch strips. (If using chicken, chop thighs into big, bite-sized chunks, and slice breast meat crosswise into 2-inch strips.) Set meat aside.

❀ In a medium saucepan or heavy skillet, bring 1 cup of the coconut milk to a gentle boil over medium-high heat. Cook for 2 to 3 minutes, until fragrant and beginning to thicken. Add the curry paste and cook 2 to 3 minutes, pressing and stirring to dissolve it into the coconut milk. Add the meat and cook 2 minutes more, tossing to coat it with the sauce.

❀ Add the remaining 2 cups coconut milk, the chicken broth, potatoes, onion, fish sauce, palm sugar, and salt and bring to a gentle boil. Reduce heat and simmer until potatoes are tender, 10 to 15 minutes. Stir in the peanuts and lime juice, transfer to a serving bowl, and serve hot or warm.

Serves 6 to 8

country-style curry with ground beef and green beans
gaeng bah neua sahp

2 tablespoons vegetable oil

1 tablespoon coarsely chopped garlic

2 tablespoons red curry paste

½ pound ground beef or ground pork

1 cup sliced fresh mushrooms

3 cups chicken broth or water

A handful of green beans, cut into 1-inch
lengths (about 1 cup)

2 medium zucchini or 2 long Asian eggplants,
halved lengthwise and cut in 1-inch lengths
(about 2 cups)

4 wild lime leaves, torn or cut into quarters
(optional)

3 tablespoons fish sauce

1 tablespoon sugar

½ teaspoon salt

A handful of holy basil (bai graprao), or other
fresh basil leaves or cilantro leaves

This firecracker version of vegetable-beef soup uses red curry paste, simmered in broth rather than coconut milk. The word bah means "forest," evoking the soup's origins, where hunters of old made curry over an open fire, without the luxurious addition of coconut milk.

Bamboo shoots, eggplant, and baby corn would make tasty additions to this hearty dish, an upcountry favorite yielding intense and fiery flavors in a flash. You could also make it with thinly sliced beef or pork, or with chicken cut in big, bite-sized chunks. Serve this curry with lots of rice and a plate of coarsely chopped tomatoes, cucumber slices, and halved hard boiled eggs. Pair it with new potatoes tossed with butter and a hunk of crusty bread for a volcanic but delicious supper on a winter night.

❀ Heat the oil in a large skillet over medium heat, add the garlic, and toss well. Add the curry paste and cook, mashing and stirring to dissolve it, until fragrant and softened, 2 to 3 minutes.

❀ Crumble in the ground beef and then add the mushrooms. Cook, tossing often, until the meat and mushrooms are browned and seasoned with the curry paste, 2 to 3 minutes.

❀ Add the chicken broth, green beans, zucchini, lime leaves (if using), fish sauce, sugar, and salt and bring to a gentle boil. Cook 3 to 5 minutes, until the vegetables are tender and the meat is cooked. Stir in the basil leaves and remove from heat. Transfer to a serving dish and serve hot or warm.

Serves 4 to 6

red curry beef with butternut squash
gaeng peht neua

1½ cups unsweetened coconut milk

2 tablespoons red curry paste

¾ pound boneless beef, such as tri-tip, flank steak, or rib-eye, thinly sliced crosswise into 2-inch strips

1½ cups chicken broth or water

1 small butternut squash, peeled and cut in generous bite-sized chunks (about 2 cups)

2 tablespoons fish sauce

1 tablespoon palm sugar or brown sugar

I love this curry; it is the first one I tasted in Thailand, the first one I made with success back home in the United States, and the first Thai dish our daughter Camellia embraced and learned to cook.

You need only the Thai pantry essentials I was able to find in a Korean market in North Carolina even years ago: red curry paste, fish sauce, palm sugar, coconut milk, and jasmine rice. Thais love red curry with chicken and bamboo shoots as well, and call it gaeng daeng *as well as* gaeng peht; daeng *meaning "red," and* peht *meaning "chili-hot." Acorn squash, kabocha pumpkin, or sweet potato chunks make delicious substitutes for butternut squash.*

❁ In a medium saucepan or heavy skillet, bring about ¾ cup of the coconut milk to a gentle boil over medium-high heat. Cook for 2 to 3 minutes, until it begins to thicken and becomes fragrant. Add the curry paste and cook 2 to 3 minutes, pressing and stirring to dissolve it into the coconut milk. Add the beef and cook another minute or two, tossing to coat it with the sauce.

❁ Add the remaining ¾ cups of coconut milk, the chicken broth, butternut squash, fish sauce, and palm sugar, and bring to a full boil. Reduce heat to maintain a lively simmer and cook, stirring now and then, until the beef is cooked and the butternut squash is tender but still firm, 5 to 7 minutes. Remove from the heat, transfer to a serving dish, and serve hot or warm.

Serves 4 to 6

red curry shrimp with pineapple
gaeng kua goong sapparote

1½ cups unsweetened coconut milk

2 tablespoons *gaeng kua* curry paste or red curry paste

½ cup water

2 tablespoons fish sauce

1 tablespoon sugar

1 cup drained canned pineapple chunks or crushed pineapple or bite-sized chunks fresh pineapple

6 wild lime leaves, quartered (optional)

¾ pound large shrimp

⅓ cup fresh Asian or Italian basil leaves, plus basil sprigs for garnish

This pleasing curry goes together in a few minutes' time. Follow this as a guideline for making a curry with seafood or fish and any curry paste you like. The base for gaeng kua *is a red curry paste made without the roasted cumin, coriander, and other spices ground into the standard red curry paste. Wild lime leaves are traditional, but if you cannot find them, you will still have a wonderful dish. Fresh pineapple is lovely, but canned pineapple works fine, too. With jasmine rice, nests of thin rice noodles or angel hair pasta, and a green salad, this makes an elegant little meal.*

In a medium skillet or saucepan, heat ½ cup of the coconut milk over medium-high heat, stirring often, until thickened and fragrant, 2 to 3 minutes. Add the curry paste and cook a minute or two, pressing and stirring to dissolve it. Stir in remaining 1 cup coconut milk, the water, fish sauce, sugar, pineapple, and lime leaves (if using), and bring to a gentle boil. Add the shrimp and basil leaves and cook another minute or two, just until shrimp are pink and cooked through. Transfer to a serving dish, garnish with fresh basil sprigs, and serve hot or warm.

Serves 4

chicken & eggs

INTRODUCTION TO CHICKEN & EGGS

Which came first, the chicken or the egg? Chicken comes first in this chapter, with a simple stir-fried dish for your stovetop, followed by a pair of Thai favorite chicken dishes, one cooked in an electric rice cooker and the other on the grill. Each is hearty, simple, and superb. I keep a package of chicken thighs and another of boneless chicken breast in the freezer, so that I can raid the icebox for one of these quick and tasty Thai chicken dishes when the grocery store seems an ocean away.

After my first few weeks of living in the Thai countryside and eating Thai food all the time, it occurred to me that the Thai appetite for eggs does not wither at the end of brunch. Thai cooks do not seem to know about the twenty-foot-tall fence separating breakfast from the rest of the day's food. Long ago they figured out that eggs are the ultimate quick-and-easy ingredient, ready in minutes, substantial and satisfying, widely available, beautiful in many guises, and good with or without a lot of kitchen fuss. They eat eggs all day and into the night. They are smart.

At my house we have Easy Omelet with Sri Rachaa Sauce (page 59) at almost every party. We jazz up leftover rice with an over-easy egg when we need a quick, late-night supper. We think Crispy Omelet with Oysters and Bean Sprouts (page 60) is incredibly delicious, and we are trying to think of the best way to bring Thai flavors to deviled eggs.

Include a few of these egg dishes in your repertoire; they give you more choices for good fast food, and they round out a Thai party menu perfectly. You can even enjoy them for breakfast or brunch.

chicken with fresh basil
gai paht bai graprao

3 tablespoons vegetable oil

1 tablespoon coarsely chopped garlic

½ cup coarsely chopped onion

¾ pound boneless chicken, coarsely ground or cut into bite-sized pieces

2 tablespoons fish sauce

1 tablespoon dark soy sauce or soy sauce

2 tablespoons water

2 teaspoons sugar

2 tablespoons coarsely chopped fresh hot green chilies, such as Thai chilies, serranos, or jalapeños

1 cup fresh holy basil (*bai graprao*), Asian basil, or Italian basil leaves or fresh mint leaves

This is my husband Will's favorite Thai dish, perhaps because he encountered it in a small cafe overlooking the Kwae River during his first journey to Thailand. Restaurant cooks make it with minced chicken, beef, or pork, hand-chopping the meat with a heavy cleaver just before cooking. Chopping the meat provides maximum surface area to absorb the spectacular combination of hot green chilies, garlic, and holy basil (bai graprao), a pungent, peppery herb. Try this using ground meat from the grocery store, or cut any other meat into bite-sized pieces, or use shrimp, decreasing the cooking time since they cook so quickly. Don't worry if you can't find holy basil, since Asian basil, Italian basil, and fresh mint make delicious substitutes. Look for holy basil seeds in Asian markets in springtime, as the plant will thrive in the West in the summer sun.

❀ Heat the oil in a large deep skillet over medium-high heat and then add the garlic and onion. Toss well, and when they begin to release their aroma, add the chicken in generous pinches. Toss well, using a spatula or slotted spoon, to help meat brown evenly and to break up big chunks to achieve a crumbly texture.

❀ Add the fish sauce, soy sauce, water, and sugar and cook 2 to 3 minutes, tossing now and then, just until the meat is cooked and the seasonings form a thin, smooth sauce. Add the chilies and basil and toss well. Transfer to a serving plate and serve hot or warm.

Serves 4

chicken hidden in curried rice
kao moke gai

3 tablespoons vegetable oil

1 tablespoon coarsely chopped garlic

⅓ cup coarsely chopped onion

1 tablespoon curry powder or ground spice
mixture (see headnote)

1½ teaspoons salt

½ teaspoon freshly ground pepper

6 chicken thighs or legs or a combination of
both (about 1½ pounds)

2 cups long-grain rice

2½ cups chicken broth or water if using
electric rice cooker, or 3½ cups chicken
broth or water if cooked on the stove

3 tablespoons coarsely chopped fresh cilantro

Optional Accompaniments

⅓ cup thinly sliced shallots, fried in vegetable
oil until golden brown and crisp, or 2 tablespoons thinly sliced green onions

Tangy Cucumber Pickles (page 128) or
cucumber slices

You will be amazed at the gorgeous color and satisfying flavor of this terrific Thai party dish. Made in an electric rice cooker, it is incredibly easy to prepare. It's also versatile: it keeps for an hour or so while you visit with your guests, or you can easily transport it to a potluck meal. Southern Thailand's adaptation of the classic biryanis of India, it can be made with boneless chicken thighs or chicken breast cut into large chunks.

If your curry powder has been in your cupboard since the last century, treat yourself to a new jar. I guarantee you will use it more often once you know how to make this delicious kao moke gai. *If you love spices, mix up a little bowl of the following ground spice mixture and use it instead of curry powder: 1 teaspoon each of ground cumin, coriander, and turmeric, and ½ teaspoon each of ground cinnamon and dried red chilies.*

❀   Place a medium bowl and tongs by the stove and heat the oil in a large skillet over medium heat. Add the garlic and onion and toss well. Sprinkle in the curry powder, along with the salt and pepper. Cook 1 minute, stir well, and then add the chicken pieces. Cook 2 to 3 minutes, turning once or twice, until they are coated with spices and beginning to brown. Transfer the partially cooked chicken pieces to the bowl and add the rice to the skillet. Cook 2 to 3 minutes, stirring now and then to evenly color and season the rice.

❀   To cook in an electric rice cooker: Put half the rice in a large rice cooker and place the chicken and any juices from the bowl on top of the rice. Scatter the rest of the rice over the chicken pieces, and then pour in the 2½ cups chicken broth. Cover, press the start button, and cook until rice and chicken are tender and cooked through, around 40 minutes, depending on your machine.

❀ To cook on the stove: Transfer the seasoned rice to a large saucepan or Dutch oven, and add the 3½ cups chicken broth. Bring to a boil over medium heat, stir well, and cook, stirring often, until the rice swells and looks rather dry, 10 to 15 minutes. Reduce heat to medium-low and add the chicken pieces to the pan, along with any juices from the bowl. Use a spoon to bury them one by one near the bottom of the pan, under the partially cooked rice. Smooth out the rice to hide the chicken completely, cover, and cook until rice is tender and chicken is cooked through, about 40 to 50 minutes, stirring gently once or twice.

❀ For either cooking method: When rice and chicken are cooked, let stand, covered, for 10 minutes. Fluff the rice gently and then mound it on a serving platter. Arrange chicken pieces around the mound of rice, garnish with the cilantro and any of the optional accompaniments, and serve hot or warm.

Serves 6 to 8

grilled garlic chicken, issahn style
gai yahng

3 tablespoons coarsely chopped fresh cilantro roots, or stems and leaves

3 tablespoons coarsely chopped garlic

1 teaspoon freshly ground pepper

2 tablespoons soy sauce

1 tablespoon fish sauce

1 teaspoon salt

3 tablespoons water, or more as needed to grind the paste

3 pounds chicken pieces

Sweet-Hot Garlic Sauce (page 129), for dipping

In Bangkok alleys and upcountry markets, at rural bus stations and outside boxing arenas, street-vendors do a brisk business in gai yahng, *the classic northeastern Thai dish. In Thailand, it's finger food, served with* nahm jeem gratiem, *Sweet-Hot Garlic Sauce (page 129), for dipping. Paired with* som tum, *Green Papaya Salad (page 121), and a generous serving of* kao niow, *Sticky Rice (page 98), it anchors the quintessential* Issahn *meal. You can marinate the chicken for more than an hour, even overnight in the refrigerator if you wish. I like to use legs and thighs, or all wings when I want finger food for a party.*

❀ In a small food processor or a blender, combine the cilantro, garlic, pepper, soy sauce, fish sauce, salt, and water. Grind to a fine, fairly smooth paste. Add another tablespoon or two of water if needed to help grind evenly. You can also mince the garlic and cilantro finely, mash them with the salt on your cutting board, and scrape the mixture into a bowl to mix with the pepper, fish sauce, and soy sauce.

❀ Transfer the paste to a large, deep mixing bowl and add the chicken pieces, turning to coat everything well. Cover and refrigerate at least an hour or even overnight, turning occasionally to coat evenly with the marinade.

❀ Prepare a very hot fire in a charcoal grill, or heat a gas grill or oven to 450 degrees F. When hot, place the chicken on the lightly oiled rack, or in a roasting pan in the oven, and cook, turning occasionally to brown and cook pieces evenly, until chicken is cooked through. Serve hot, warm, or at room temperature, with small bowls of Sweet-Hot Garlic Sauce.

Serves 4 to 6

chicken with cashews and chilies
gai paht meht mamuang himapahn

3 tablespoons vegetable oil

2 large dried red chilies, each cut into 4 pieces, or 6 to 8 small dried red chilies

¾ pound boneless chicken thighs or breast, cut into bite-sized chunks

1 medium onion, cut lengthwise into thick wedges (about 1 cup)

2 tablespoons fish sauce

2 tablespoons water

2 teaspoons soy sauce

½ teaspoon sugar

½ cup dry-roasted, salted cashews

This fabulous combination of juicy chunks of chicken and plump, luscious cashew nuts is my father's favorite Thai dish, his order every time we eat at a Thai restaurant. In Chinese restaurants he goes for the chicken with almonds, a good nut to substitute in this simple recipe if you don't have cashews. Though Daddy served in the Marine Corps and is the bravest man I know, he doesn't care for hot, spicy food, so for him I leave the chilies out. You can also moderate the heat by decreasing the amount of dried chilies you use.

You can find dried red chilies in Mexican markets as well as Asian markets. Look for Anaheim, New Mexico, and California chilies if you want big, milder ones, and chiles japones and chiles de arbol if you want the small, fiery ones. Asian markets carry dried red chilies, too, but labels often omit the variety. They all work fine; just remember that the smaller the chili, the hotter its flavor will be.

❀ Set a serving platter by the stove and have a slotted spoon or spatula and a saucer handy for removing the chilies before they burn. Heat the oil for about 1 minute in a deep, heavy skillet over medium heat, and then add the chilies. Toss and cook for about 1 minute, letting them darken a bit but taking care not to let them blacken and burn. Scoop out the chilies and set aside.

❀ Increase the heat to medium-high and add the chicken. Cook until it changes color, 1 to 2 minutes. Add the onion and stir-fry about 2 minutes more, until the onion softens and becomes shiny and the chicken is cooked through. Add the fish sauce, water, soy sauce, and sugar and toss well. Add the cashews and the reserved chilies and cook 1 more minute, tossing once or twice. Transfer to a serving platter and serve hot or warm.

Serves 4

easy omelet with sri rachaa sauce
kai jiow

4 eggs

1 tablespoon fish sauce

1 tablespoon water

2 tablespoons vegetable oil

Sri Rachaa sauce, Tabasco sauce,
  or other hot sauce

Whenever we invite company over for Thai food, this simple dish goes on the menu first thing. Quick, easy, satisfying, and made from the simplest ingredients, it looks tasty and familiar to guests who are new to Asian food. Need I add that kids love it, old folks love it, I love it, and there is seldom any left to put away at the end of the feast? If you make it in a wok with a little extra oil, it will puff up grandly, but this doesn't last and it tastes wonderful even flat as the proverbial pancake. Thais serve it with a saucer of crimson Sri Rachaa sauce, which provides some heat for those who like it. For a heartier version, stir in a little ground pork and some chopped tomatoes when you beat the eggs. For a vegetarian version, replace the fish sauce with lime juice and add chopped cilantro, green onions, and a generous pinch of salt.

❀ Combine the eggs, fish sauce, and water in a medium bowl and use a fork or a whisk to blend them well. Heat the oil in a medium skillet or a wok over medium-high heat until a bit of the egg mixture sizzles and blooms at once.

❀ Pour in the eggs and as soon as they begin to set, pull the puffy edges gently toward the center, letting the uncooked eggs in the center flow out to the edges and cook. When the edges are golden and the surface is almost set, gently flip the omelet to cook the other side for 1 minute. Don't worry if it breaks; it will still be delicious.

❀ Scoop the omelet out onto a serving plate, and serve at once with small saucers of Sri Rachaa sauce.

Serves 4 to 6

crispy omelet with oysters and bean sprouts
hoi tote

¼ cup rice flour or cornstarch

¼ cup tapioca flour or all-purpose flour

1 teaspoon salt

½ cup water

2 eggs

3 tablespoons vegetable oil

½ to ¾ cup shelled fresh oysters or
   mussels (about ½ pound) or
   12 shelled medium shrimp

1½ cups fresh bean sprouts

2 or 3 green onions, white part finely chopped
   and green part chopped into 1-inch lengths

¼ cup coarsely chopped fresh cilantro

⅓ cup Sri Rachaa sauce, Tabasco sauce, or
   other hot sauce (optional)

Here is the kind of dish that gives street food a good name. You scatter a simple batter on a hot griddle to form a lacy noodle pancake. Oysters go on next, or mussels, or shrimp, and then eggs, green onions, and bean sprouts, all to be tumbled into a luscious, salty seafood feast. Thais do not generally make this at home, and why would they? They can stroll to the night market and stand in line at a hoi tote *vendor's griddle with a few* baht *and a lean hungry look. But if they come West and get homesick, they will find that* hoi tote *is quick, delicious, and easy to make.*

The two special types of flour used (rice and tapioca) are easy to find in Asian markets, and they keep forever. Transfer the opened bags to a large resealable plastic bag and keep them in your pantry. Rest assured that an equal combination of cornstarch and all-purpose flour makes a good substitute.

❀ In a small bowl, combine the rice flour, tapioca flour, ½ teaspoon of the salt, and the water and stir well. In another small bowl, lightly beat the eggs with the remaining ½ teaspoon salt. Place both the eggs and the batter by the stove, along with a serving platter.

❀ In a large, flat skillet over medium-high heat, heat the oil until a bit of the flour batter sizzles at once. Using a ladle or a large spoon, splash in the batter, using only enough to form a big, lacy, open pancake. Scatter the oysters over the pancake and let cook 1 to 2 minutes, until the pancake is fairly firm and crisp. Splash the eggs unevenly over the pancake and oysters, and let everything cook 1 minute longer, until the eggs are almost set.

❀ Use a spatula to chop the pancake in half down the middle, and then turn each half over. Breaks don't matter—this dish is a glorious delicious mess. Make space in the middle of the skillet for the bean sprouts and green onions. Cook 1 to 2 minutes more, tossing the vegetables until they are shiny and fragrant.

❀ Scoop up the bean sprouts and green onions and mound them on one side of a serving platter. Pile the two big pieces of the omelet onto the middle and other side of the platter. Sprinkle with cilantro, and serve hot or warm, with a small bowl of Sri Rachaa sauce.

Serves 2 to 4

son-in-law eggs with crispy shallots

kai leuk koey

Tamarind Sauce

¾ cup tamarind liquid (see page 150) or Indian-style tamarind chutney or freshly squeezed lime juice

¼ cup palm sugar or brown sugar

¼ cup fish sauce

¼ cup water

Eggs and Crispy Shallots

Vegetable oil for frying eggs

6 eggs, hard-boiled, shelled, and patted dry

¼ cup thinly sliced shallots

2 teaspoons coarsely chopped dried red chili flakes

3 tablespoons coarsely chopped fresh cilantro leaves

I like hard-boiled eggs any way you serve them, but I adore them in this magnificent party dish. Fried to a golden brown, halved and arranged on a platter, the eggs are sprinkled with crispy rings of fried shallots and napped with a stupendous sweet-and-tangy sauce of tamarind, fish sauce, and palm sugar. It is glorious, and although Son-in-Law Eggs are often served at Thai wedding celebrations and Buddhist ordination feasts, they are simple to make.

Indian-style tamarind chutney is an excellent short-cut to make use of when preparing this sauce. You'll often find it among the Indian ingredients on well-stocked supermarket shelves, or check the mail order sources (page 162) or in Middle Eastern and South Asian groceries. If frying the hard-boiled eggs seems over the top to you, simply skip that step; the dish will still be superb. Serve Son-in-Law Eggs with rice, couscous, thin rice noodles, or triangles of toast. You will love having something substantial with which to savor the delicious sauce.

✳ To prepare the sauce, combine the tamarind liquid, palm sugar, fish sauce, and water in a medium saucepan and bring to a gentle boil over medium heat. Lower heat to maintain a lively simmer and cook 4 to 5 minutes to make a smooth, delicate syrup, stirring once or twice, and then transfer to a small bowl to cool.

continued

❀ To fry the eggs and crispy shallots, line a tray or two plates with paper towels, and set a slotted spoon or a pair of spatulas by the stove. Heat about 3 inches of vegetable oil in a medium skillet or wok over medium heat to frying temperature, 350 to 375 degrees F. When a bit of shallot sizzles at once, carefully lower 3 of the eggs into the oil and fry, turning to cook them evenly, until golden brown and crisp all over, 5 to 7 minutes. Remove and drain on paper towels, and repeat with the remaining 3 eggs. Scatter the shallots into the skillet and fry 1 to 2 minutes, until handsomely browned but not burned. Remove and drain on paper towels.

❀ To serve, halve the eggs lengthwise and arrange on a serving platter. Pour the tamarind sauce over eggs, sprinkle them with the crispy shallots, chili flakes, and cilantro, and serve warm or at room temperature.

Serves 4 to 6

five-spice stew with hard-boiled eggs and pork
kai pa-loh

2 tablespoons vegetable oil

2 tablespoons finely chopped garlic

2 tablespoons finely chopped fresh cilantro
roots, or stems and leaves, plus 2 tablespoons
coarsely chopped fresh cilantro leaves

1 tablespoon five-spice powder

½ teaspoon freshly ground black pepper

½ pound boneless pork or beef, thinly sliced
across the grain into 2-inch strips

4 cups chicken broth or water

3 tablespoons dark soy sauce or soy sauce

3 tablespoons palm sugar or brown sugar

1 teaspoon salt

6 hard-boiled eggs, peeled

I adore this satisfying stew, redolent with spices and with nary a hint of chili heat. Pong pa-loh is the Thai name for five-spice powder. Widely available in supermarkets as well Asian groceries, it provides a deep, rich flavor to this classic Chinese-Thai comfort food. The cinnamon, cloves, and fennel seed seem familiar, while the star anise and Szechuan peppercorns provide an exotic note. Using thinly sliced pork or beef makes the dish quick and easy; the traditional version calls for stewing fresh ham for hours in the aromatic, coffee-colored broth. You could also use meatballs made from ground pork or beef, or 6 chicken legs or thighs, with delicious results. Serve it on a wintry day with Tangy Cucumber Pickles (page 128) and lots of rice or noodles. Refrigerate any leftovers; you will see that it tastes even better the next day.

❀ In a medium saucepan over medium-high heat, combine the oil, garlic, and cilantro roots and cook, tossing often, until sizzling and fragrant, about 1 minute. Sprinkle in the five-spice powder and the pepper and toss well. Add the pork and toss well to season it with the spice mixture. Add the chicken broth, soy sauce, palm sugar, salt, and eggs, and bring to a boil. Reduce heat to maintain a lively simmer and cook 30 minutes, stirring now and then to color eggs evenly. Remove from heat, take out the eggs, halve them lengthwise, and return them to the stew. Transfer to a serving bowl, sprinkle with cilantro leaves, and serve hot or warm with rice or over noodles.

Serves 6 to 8

meats

INTRODUCTION TO MEATS

For a land where meat plays a minor role compared to fish, chicken, and soy foods, Thai people certainly know how to cook it well. Beef stir-fried simply with oyster sauce and crisp broccoli florets shows its Chinese origins, and beef sautéed with red curry paste, garlic, and fragrant basil leaves tells the world that Thai food is feisty, complex, and unlike any other. When you crave fiery flavors, you can grill up some Crying Tiger Steak, and when you need an incentive to eat your vegetables, just cook up a skilletful of green beans with pork Thai-style, sweet, spicy, and hot.

Three of the dishes in this chapter come from the rustic cuisine of northeastern Thailand, known as *pahk Issahn*, where robust meat dishes stand out, fearlessly seasoned with chilies, sharp notes of citrus, and the crunch of coarsely ground roasted rice. You can use most any cut of beef you like in these hearty dishes; flank steak and tri-tip are particularly good for stir-fried dishes, especially if you place the meat in the freezer and slice it thinly while still partially frozen. All these dishes will serve four people nicely, if you provide lots of rice and another dish or two to round out the meal.

beef with broccoli in oyster sauce
neua paht naman hoy

2 tablespoons vegetable oil

1 tablespoon coarsely chopped garlic

½ pound boneless beef, such as tri-tip or
   flank steak, thinly sliced crosswise into
   2-inch strips

¾ pound broccoli florets, halved lengthwise
   unless very small

2 tablespoons oyster sauce

2 tablespoons fish sauce

1 teaspoon sugar

½ teaspoon freshly ground pepper

⅓ cup water

Thais make this dish with pahk ka-nah, *a sturdy, delectable cousin of broccoli that is longer on leaves and shorter on flowers. Its Cantonese name is* gai-lan, *and its leaves easily pass for collard greens, in color and texture though not in size. If* pahk ka-nah *is not handy,* mai pen rai—*never mind! Grab your favorite leafy green, be it spinach, Swiss chard (red or green), beet greens, rapini, Napa cabbage, or bok choy, or use broccoli, as I have here. All are good, all are good for you, and any would work well in this dish. If you use spinach, add it toward the end of cooking, so that its delicate leaves have a mere 2 minutes or so in the hot pan.*

Heat the oil in a deep, heavy skillet or wok over medium-high heat until a bit of garlic sizzles at once. Add the garlic and toss well. Then add the beef and toss until it changes color. Add the broccoli florets and toss for about 1 minute, until they turn shiny and bright green. Add the oyster sauce, fish sauce, sugar, pepper, and water and cook 3 to 4 minutes, tossing often, until broccoli is tender and beef is cooked. Transfer to a small serving platter and serve hot or warm.

Serves 4

beef and zucchini in red curry sauce
neua paht peht

2 tablespoons vegetable oil

1 tablespoon coarsely chopped garlic

2 tablespoons red curry paste or another Thai curry paste

½ pound boneless beef, such as tri-tip or flank steak, thinly sliced crosswise into 2-inch strips

2 medium zucchini, halved lengthwise and cut crosswise into 1-inch pieces (about 1½ cups)

½ cup water

2 tablespoons fish sauce

1 tablespoon palm sugar

About ½ cup fresh basil leaves or fresh mint leaves, plus sprigs for garnish (optional)

Thais cook beef, pork, and crisp-fried freshwater fish in this rustic style. Untamed by the velvet cushioning of coconut milk, curry paste reveals its wild side here—a fascinating and welcome presence, provided you offer abundant plain rice to maintain order. Red curry paste and holy basil are classic in paht peht, *but you can use any Thai curry paste and any variety of fresh basil or mint. A flourish of fresh cilantro or a handful of chopped green onions will work as well. I love the cut of beef called "tri-tip" in stir-fried dishes like this one, but flank steak works well, and so does any nicely marbled steak, fat and all. Then there's chicken, ground beef, or ground pork if you need to get supper into the pan really fast.*

✼ In a large, deep skillet or a wok, heat the oil over medium heat. Add the garlic and when it is sizzling and fragrant, add the curry paste. Reduce heat to low and cook gently for about 2 minutes, mashing and stirring to melt the paste into the oil.

✼ Add the beef and toss to coat it with curry paste. Stir in the zucchini, and then add the water, fish sauce, and palm sugar. Cook, stirring now and then, until the zucchini is tender and the sauce is smooth, 2 to 3 minutes. Stir in the basil leaves, transfer to a small serving platter, and garnish with basil sprigs, if using. Serve hot or warm.

Serves 4

crying tiger steak with roasted tomato–chili sauce
seua rohng hai gahp jaew makeua-teht

Marinade for Steak

2 tablespoons soy sauce

1 tablespoon fish sauce

1 teaspoon sugar

1 pound boneless beef steak, such as rib eye, strip, or flank steak

Roasted Tomato–Chili Sauce

5 small dried red chilies, or 1 tablespoon coarsely ground dried red chili flakes

½ cup very coarsely chopped onion

3 large cloves garlic, very coarsely chopped

12 cherry tomatoes, or a generous ½ cup of quartered plum or roma tomatoes

⅓ cup fish sauce

¼ cup lime juice or white vinegar

3 tablespoons sugar

So what is the story on that whimsical name for this robust Issahn-style restaurant classic? Is the dipping sauce really so spicy it would make a Thai tiger cry? Does fat from the lusciously marbled beef steak indeed melt onto fiery coals and flame up like a tiger's tears? Could not both these tales be true? See, the tiger snatches a pawful or two of Roasted Tomato–Chili Sauce, bursts into tears, and then weeps uncontrollably over a temporarily unmonitored charcoal grill.

We do not have an answer to this mystery at press time, but I do know this: The steak marinates a mere hour, and the dipping sauce is fantastic, great on sandwiches and noodles even after the steak is gone. I therefore recommend that you make the dish while keeping those tigers at bay. Soak and steam up some Sticky Rice (page 98) if you can; it is perfect here. If you are short on time for making the sauce, use Sweet-Hot Garlic Sauce (page 129) or stir together three tablespoons of fish sauce, two of lime juice, and one of sugar and then spike it with a little chopped fresh cilantro and some ground dried red chili flakes.

In a medium bowl, prepare the marinade by combining the soy sauce, fish sauce, and sugar. Add the steak, turning to coat it, and let stand 30 minutes to 1 hour, turning now and then.

To make the sauce, dry-fry the whole chilies in a large skillet over medium heat for about 1 minute, until darkened and fragrant but not burnt. Scoop them out onto a plate, increase the heat to medium-high, and dry-fry the onion, garlic, and tomatoes, turning now and then, until nicely browned but not burnt, about 2 minutes. (If you use dried red chili flakes, add them when the tomato mixture is almost ready; they burn fast.) Scoop everything out

continued

onto the plate, break the whole chilies into pieces, and set aside. Combine the fish sauce, lime juice, and sugar in the jar of a blender or a small food processor. Add the roasted tomato mixture and pulse everything to form a thick, fairly smooth sauce; stop while some chili bits and seeds are still visible in the sauce. Transfer to a small bowl and set aside.

❀ Prepare a very hot fire in a charcoal grill, or heat a gas grill or oven to 450 degrees F. When hot, place the meat on the lightly oiled rack, or in a roasting pan in the oven, and cook, turning as needed, until richly browned outside and done to your liking. Let it stand on the serving platter for about 5 minutes. Transfer to a cutting board, slice against the grain into thick strips, and arrange on a serving platter with any juices poured over the steak. Serve warm or at room temperature, with Roasted Tomato–Chili Sauce.

Serves 4 to 6

panaeng beef in red curry peanut sauce
panaeng neua

1 cup unsweetened coconut milk

½ cup water

½ pound boneless beef, such as flank steak or tri-tip, thinly sliced crosswise into 2-inch strips

2 tablespoons *panaeng* curry paste or red curry paste

2 tablespoons fish sauce

2 tablespoons palm sugar or brown sugar

3 tablespoons ground or finely chopped peanuts or peanut butter

3 wild lime leaves, torn or cut in quarters or fine threads (optional)

A handful of Thai or Italian basil leaves, plus a few sprigs for garnish (optional)

One of Thailand's signature dishes, panaeng neua *is extraordinary: flat-out delicious, and easier, much easier, than pie. With jasmine rice and a great big green salad, this makes a memorable meal. To grind peanuts for this recipe, use your spice grinder, pulsing on and off to grind evenly, or mince them well with your big knife. Natural-food stores often have grind-it-yourself peanut butter contraptions, but take heart: school lunch peanut butter will also work. The classic presentation for* panaeng *dishes is on a shallow platter, topped with a splash of thick coconut milk, threads of lime leaves, and shreds of hot red peppers scattered over the gorgeous sauce. Make this even if you don't have fresh basil or wild lime leaves; it will still be absolutely delicious. If you have wild lime leaves and a little extra time, snip them into wire-thin threads, cutting crosswise with kitchen scissors, or roll them into little cylinders and cut into very thin strips.*

In a medium saucepan, stir together ½ cup of the coconut milk and the water and bring to a very gentle boil over medium heat. Sprinkle in the sliced beef, stirring to keep the pieces from sticking together, and simmer 5 minutes, until meat is tender. With a slotted spoon, scoop the meat out into a bowl and set aside, leaving coconut milk in pan to return to a gentle boil. Stir in the curry paste and cook, pressing and stirring to dissolve the paste, 3 to 4 minutes, until the sauce is fragrant and smooth. Return the beef and any juices to the pan, add the remaining ½ cup coconut milk, and bring back to a gentle boil. Add the fish sauce, palm sugar, peanuts, and lime leaves, if using. Stir well and simmer 3 to 4 minutes more, until the sauce is smooth. Stir in the basil leaves and remove from heat. Transfer to a small platter, garnish with a flourish of basil sprigs, if using, and serve hot or warm.

Serves 4 to 6

grilled beef salad with chilies and lime
yum neua yahng

1 pound boneless beef steak, such as rib eye, strip, or flank, grilled medium-rare

⅓ cup chicken broth

3 tablespoons fish sauce

3 tablespoons freshly squeezed lime juice

2 teaspoons sugar

2 teaspoons coarsely ground dried red chili flakes

2 tablespoons finely chopped shallots

2 green onions, thinly sliced crosswise

A handful of fresh cilantro leaves, coarsely chopped

A handful of fresh mint leaves, coarsely chopped, plus a few sprigs for garnish

Thais serve this hearty dish with lettuce, tomatoes, and slices of cucumber. With Sticky Rice (page 98), it can be the centerpiece of a simple but exotic picnic. Grilled beef left over from last night's cookout (see Crying Tiger Steak, page 71) is the perfect start for this recipe, but you could also cook the beef just before you prepare the dish, on the grill, under the broiler, or in a skillet. For the real northeastern Thai version, add a spoonful of roasted rice powder (see page 77) along with the mint.

❀ Thinly slice the beef across the grain into bite-sized strips, about 2 inches long, and set aside.

❀ In a medium saucepan, bring the chicken broth to a gentle boil over medium heat. Add the beef and stir to warm it in the hot broth, no longer than 1 minute. Remove from heat and transfer to a medium bowl.

❀ Add the fish sauce, lime juice, sugar, and chili flakes and, using your hand, mix everything together quickly and well. Add the shallots, green onions, cilantro, and chopped mint and mix again. Turn out onto a small, deep serving plate in a mound, pouring the sauce over the top, and garnish with a few sprigs of mint. Serve warm or at room temperature.

Serves 4 to 6

issahn-style minced pork salad with crunchy rice and fresh mint
lahp moo

1 tablespoon raw long-grain rice

1 cup chicken stock or water

½ pound coarsely ground pork or beef

3 tablespoons freshly squeezed lime juice

2 tablespoons fish sauce

1 to 2 teaspoons dried red chili flakes

½ teaspoon sugar

A handful of fresh mint leaves, plus a few
  sprigs for garnish

2 tablespoons thinly sliced shallots

2 heaping tablespoons thinly sliced
  green onions

Optional Accompaniments

Cabbage wedges or small lettuce leaf cups

Cucumber slices

5 green beans or 2 yard-long beans, cut into
  3-inch lengths

An Issahn classic *that has gone national and even international, this dish sparkles with the flavors and aromas of northeastern Thai food: the siren-song of lime juice, the blast of chili heat, the smoky crunch of roasted grains of rice, and the earthy perfume of shallots and fresh mint. It is a winner, worthy of its fame, and it is also a simple combination of everyday grocery-store ingredients. Thais love to use raw cabbage leaves to scoop up this hearty salad bite by bite, and balance its bright, sharp flavors with the cool crunch of cucumbers and green beans. Spoon it into small lettuce cups if you like, so that your guests can eat it out of hand, or serve it with rice as part of a meal.*

❀ Make roasted rice powder by toasting the raw rice in a small dry skillet over medium heat, stirring and tossing for 3 to 5 minutes, until it turns a wheaty golden brown. Tip out onto a plate, and then grind it to a coarse powder, using a spice grinder or mortar and pestle. Set aside.

❀ Bring the chicken stock to a boil in a medium saucepan over high heat. Crumble in the meat and cook, turning and pressing to break up larger chunks. Cook the meat evenly, 1 to 2 minutes, until cooked through. Scoop meat into a medium bowl with about ¼ cup of the broth.

continued

※ Add the roasted rice powder to the bowl along with the lime juice, fish sauce, chili flakes, and sugar, and use your hands to mix everything well. Tear the mint leaves in half, add to the bowl along with the shallots and green onions, and mix well. Mound the salad on a small, deep serving platter, juices and all, and garnish with the mint sprigs and with any of the optional accompaniments. Serve at room temperature.

Serves 4 to 6

pork with spicy green beans
moo paht prik king

½ pound fresh green beans or Asian yard-long beans, cut into 2-inch lengths (about 2 cups)

3 tablespoons vegetable oil

3 tablespoons *prik king* curry paste or red curry paste

2 tablespoons dried shrimp, finely chopped or ground (optional)

¼ pound pork, thinly sliced crosswise into 2-inch strips

⅓ cup chicken stock or water

2 tablespoons fish sauce

1 tablespoon palm sugar or brown sugar

4 wild lime leaves (optional)

How could this not be one of my favorite Thai dishes? I grew up in North Carolina eating my grandmother's green beans cooked with pork, sans chilies of course, and my sister Linda always orders moo paht prik king *for us at Indra Thai, in Glendale, California. You can find* prik king *curry paste in Asian markets, but any red curry paste will work fine. For a traditional* prik king, *ground dried shrimp are an essential ingredient. You can buy them ground, grind them in your spice grinder, chop them finely, or leave them whole. You can also leave them out; this makes a fantastic, feisty dish with rice either way.*

❀ Bring a medium saucepan of water to a rolling boil. Add the green beans and cook 3 minutes, until tender but still crisp. Drain and set aside.

❀ Heat the oil in a large skillet over low heat, and add the *prik king* paste and dried shrimp, if using. Cook 3 to 4 minutes, pressing the curry paste and stirring as it softens and becomes fragrant. Increase the heat to medium-high and add the pork, tossing about 1 minute to coat it with sauce.

❀ Stir in the chicken stock, fish sauce, palm sugar, cooked green beans, and lime leaves, if using, and cook 2 to 3 minutes more, tossing often, until beans are heated through and sauce is well combined. Transfer to a serving dish and serve hot or warm.

Serves 4 to 6

fish & seafood

INTRODUCTION TO FISH & SEAFOOD

Rice and fish are the essential elements of Thai food. Seldom far from flowing water, be it a meandering stream or the River Chao Phraya, Thai people have always fished. They fish for their breakfast, lunch, and dinner, for a product to sell for cash at the market, for something to salt and preserve as a protein and vitamin source, and for something delicious to season their rice.

The most popular fish are *plah dook,* catfish, and *plah chon,* serpenthead fish. You will find these two on sale at nearly every upcountry market, and when you see one make the great leap out of its pink plastic tub and slither wildly toward the river, you will not need to ask if the fish is fresh.

Thais know what to do with fish: They fry it, steam it, and sauté it with red curry paste, holy basil, and clusters of fresh green peppercorns. They simmer it with lemongrass, lime juice, and chilies for *tom yum,* and they fry it and then curry it for *choo chee plah.* They dry it, pickle it, salt-cure it, and distill it down to fish sauce, which seasons every single Thai dish save the sweetest sweets. Whole fish is considered the ideal in terms of flavor and beauty, with bone-in fish steaks the next best thing. To keep these recipes simple and quick I used fillets in most cases, and the results were absolutely delicious.

Seafood is a treat, and the Thai tendency is to do as little to it as possible. Shrimp are simply stir-fried with snow peas, or sautéed with roasted chili paste (*nahm prik pao*) and fresh basil. Shrimp, squid, and saltwater fish are salted and sun-dried, then nibbled as a snack or cooked with soups and vegetables for pungent flavor.

Aside from the fact that Thai cooks have always had fish handy, the reason Thai people love to eat fish is that they make it taste fabulous. With these recipes, so can you.

catfish fillets fried with turmeric, southern style
plah toht kamin

2 tablespoons coarsely chopped garlic

1 tablespoon coarsely chopped shallots

2 teaspoons ground turmeric, or 1 heaping tablespoon coarsely chopped fresh or frozen turmeric

1 teaspoon sugar

1 teaspoon freshly ground pepper

½ teaspoon salt

2 tablespoons fish sauce

3 tablespoons vegetable oil

1 ¼ pounds firm fish fillets, such as catfish, tilapia, snapper, halibut, or black bass

About 1 cup all-purpose flour

Warm and golden as sunset on the island of Koh Samui, this spectacular dish is yours for only a bit of chopping and a few minutes at the stove. A brief time in the marinade is fine, but if you need to cover and refrigerate it for a day, no problem. Plah is Thai for "fish," and kamin means "turmeric." This dish is also called plah kluk kamin, kluk meaning "pounded in a mortar," whereas toht means "fried." If you have a mortar and pestle, you could try grinding the herbs and spices to an aromatic paste the traditional way. Serve this scrumptious fish with small bowls of fish sauce spiked with chopped fresh hot chilies or dried chili flakes.

In the workbowl of a small food processor or blender, combine the garlic, shallots, turmeric, sugar, pepper, salt, fish sauce, and 1 tablespoon of the vegetable oil. Grind to a fairly smooth paste, stopping now and then to scrape down the sides and adding a little water as needed to bring the ingredients together. In a medium bowl, combine the fish fillets with the turmeric marinade, turning to coat, and set aside for 15 minutes to 20 minutes; longer is fine, covered and refrigerated, up to 1 day.

To cook the fish, pour the flour in a deep plate. Dip fillets in flour, shake off excess, and set on a plate by stove. Heat the remaining 2 tablespoons of vegetable oil over medium-high heat until a drop of the marinade sizzles at once. Add the fish fillets and cook, carefully turning once, for 5 to 7 minutes (thicker fillets will need more time) until golden brown and cooked through. Transfer to a serving platter and serve hot or warm.

Serves 4

snapper in choo-chee curry sauce
choo-chee plah ga-pong

1¼ pounds firm fish fillets, such as snapper, grouper, catfish, tilapia, mackerel, or salmon; or shrimp, peeled and deveined

About 1 cup all-purpose flour

2 tablespoons vegetable oil

1 cup unsweetened coconut milk

2 tablespoons red curry paste, such as *gaeng kua, choo-chee, panaeng,* or *gaeng peht*

¼ cup water

2 tablespoons fish sauce

1 tablespoon palm sugar

4 wild lime leaves, cut crosswise into very fine threads or torn into quarters, or 2 tablespoons thinly sliced green onions

2 tablespoons coarsely chopped fresh cilantro

I still remember savoring this sumptuous curry with my friend Sandi in Bangkok, at Than Ying, *a lovely restaurant off Silom Road. As befits elegant palace-style cuisine, it was made with huge freshwater prawns and spiked with wild lime slivers. We swooned, and then quickly devoured every bite. Fortified, we marched back out into the sweltering April sunshine, ready to continue our mission of researching real Thai food.* Choo-chee *curries pack intense, bright flavor into a thick red curry sauce. Fish or seafood are first fried to a golden crisp and then simmered briefly in the sauce. No wonder Thai and Laotian people love to eat fish.*

❀ Cut the fish fillets crosswise into 2-inch pieces, and pour the flour into a deep plate. Dip each piece of fish in the flour and shake off the excess.

❀ Heat the vegetable oil in a large skillet over medium-high heat until a pinch of flour sizzles at once. Gently add fish fillets and cook 2 to 3 minutes on each side, until nicely browned and crisp. (They need not be completely cooked, as they will simmer in the sauce before serving.) Remove from pan and drain on paper towels. Pour off remaining oil.

❀ Warm ½ cup of the coconut milk in the skillet over medium heat until fragrant and creamy, about 3 minutes. Add the curry paste and cook, stirring to dissolve it, 3 to 4 minutes. Stir in the remaining ½ cup coconut milk, water, fish sauce, palm sugar, and half the lime leaves, and bring to a gentle boil. Add the fish and simmer 2 to 3 minutes more, spooning the curry over the fish as it cooks. Place fillets on a deep serving platter, cover with curry sauce, sprinkle with remaining lime leaves and the cilantro, and serve hot or warm.

Serves 4 to 6

easy salmon cakes
tode mun plah sah-mone grapong

1 can (14¾ ounce) pink salmon, or about
  1½ cups cooked flaked salmon

½ cup mashed potatoes or bread crumbs

¼ cup finely chopped onion

¼ cup coarsely chopped fresh cilantro, basil,
  mint, or dill

1 egg

1 tablespoon red curry paste

1 tablespoon fish sauce

½ teaspoon salt

½ teaspoon freshly ground pepper

3 tablespoons vegetable oil

We must have had salmon cakes once a week during my North Carolina child-hood, and they are still on the menu at Mama Dip's Kitchen here in Chapel Hill, North Carolina. I love them, especially now that I often need to produce a tasty supper fast without making an expedition to the store. Given my passion for Thai flavors, I naturally developed this unique version of my childhood favorite. Canned salmon is great for this, but you could make a fabulous version using flaked salmon left over from a recent feast. I like using mashed potatoes to bind the cakes together, but the Southern breadcrumb method suited my grand-mother—use whichever is easier for you. I serve these with steamed broccoli or a big green salad and jasmine rice, and pass the Sri Rachaa sauce for a little extra heat. We also love these salmon cakes tucked into a bun or a pita pocket along with lettuce and tomato, cucumber, and a dollop of mayonnaise spiked with roasted chili paste or red curry paste and chopped green onions.

❀ Drain salmon well, place it in a medium bowl, and remove and discard any bones and skin. Add the mashed potatoes, onion, and cilantro. In a small bowl stir and mash the egg, red curry paste, fish sauce, salt, and pepper until fairly smooth. Add to the salmon mixture and use your hands or a large spoon to combine everything well. Shape into six to eight 3-inch patties and set aside.

❀ Heat the oil in a large skillet over medium-high heat until a bit of the salmon mixture sizzles at once. Gently add half the salmon patties and cook, carefully turning once, until golden brown, about 3 minutes on each side. Transfer to a serving platter and cook the remaining patties the same way. Serve hot or warm.

Serves 4 to 6

grilled salmon with chili-lime sauce
plah sah-mohn pao

Fish

3 tablespoons coarsely chopped garlic

3 tablespoons coarsely chopped fresh cilantro roots, or stems and leaves

2 tablespoons fish sauce

1 tablespoon dark soy sauce or soy sauce

½ teaspoon sugar

½ teaspoon salt

½ teaspoon freshly ground pepper

2 tablespoons vegetable oil

1½ pounds meaty fish fillets, such as salmon, tuna, snapper, cod, halibut, catfish, or tilapia

Sauce

¼ cup fish sauce

3 tablespoons freshly squeezed lime juice

2 tablespoons sugar

1 teaspoon finely chopped garlic

1 teaspoon finely chopped fresh hot green chilies

1 teaspoon finely chopped fresh cilantro

Thais often mash garlic, cilantro roots, and whole peppercorns in a heavy mortar to make an aromatic seasoning paste. You can use a blender or small-capacity food processor, or simply mince the herbs finely with your big knife, mash them on your cutting board with the salt using the back of a large spoon, and then stir them in with the other seasonings. Use bone-in fish steaks if you like, allowing a bit more cooking time. This is tasty fried or baked in a hot oven—it is just plain good.

❁ To prepare the fish: In the workbowl of a small food processor or a blender, combine the garlic, cilantro roots, fish sauce, soy sauce, sugar, salt, pepper, and oil. Grind to a fairly smooth paste, stopping now and then to scrape down the sides and adding a little water as needed to bring the ingredients together. Scrape the cilantro-garlic paste into a medium bowl, add the fish fillets, and toss to coat everything well. Set aside for 20 to 30 minutes; longer is fine, covered and refrigerated, up to 1 day.

❁ To make the sauce: Combine the fish sauce, lime juice, sugar, and garlic in a small bowl. Stir well until the sugar dissolves, and then sprinkle with the chilies and cilantro. Set aside until serving time.

❁ Prepare a very hot fire in a charcoal grill, or heat a gas grill or oven to 425 degrees F. To cook the fish, place it on a lightly oiled grill rack, or in a shallow baking pan in the oven. Cook until handsomely browned and done to your liking, carefully turning once, about 5 minutes on each side, or longer for thicker fillets. Serve hot or warm, with the bowl of sauce on the side.

Serves 4 to 6

pan-seared tuna with green curry sauce
plah tu-nah laht gaeng kiow wahn

Fish

1 tablespoon fish sauce

1 tablespoon soy sauce

1 teaspoon sugar

¼ teaspoon freshly ground pepper

1½ pounds tuna, salmon, or other meaty
   fish steaks

Curry Sauce

1 cup unsweetened coconut milk

2 tablespoons curry paste

2 tablespoons fish sauce

1 tablespoon palm sugar or brown sugar

2 tablespoons vegetable oil

Here the tuna marinates while you simmer up a vibrant curry sauce, complex in flavor but simple in every other way. Use any curry paste, from green to yellow to mussamun. The sauce is also terrific with grilled shrimp, roast chicken, or new potatoes and peas. Stir the canned coconut milk well before measuring it out, as it naturally separates as it stands. You can make the sauce ahead and reheat it gently close to serving time.

❀ In a medium bowl, stir together the fish sauce, soy sauce, sugar, and pepper. Place the fish steaks in the bowl, turn to coat them well, and let them marinate for 20 to 30 minutes, turning once; longer is fine, covered and refrigerated, up to 1 day.

❀ To prepare the curry sauce: Bring the coconut milk to a gentle boil in a medium skillet over medium heat. Simmer 3 to 4 minutes, until it is fragrant and has thickened a bit. Add the curry paste and cook, mashing and stirring now and then, until the paste dissolves and becomes fragrant, 3 to 4 minutes. Stir in the fish sauce and palm sugar, and remove from heat. Set aside while you cook the fish.

❀ Heat the vegetable oil in a large skillet over medium-high heat, and add the tuna steaks. Lower heat to medium and cook about 5 minutes on each side, or until done to your taste. Pour the curry sauce into a deep serving plate, place tuna steaks on the sauce, and serve hot or warm.

Serves 4 to 6

quick red curry with tuna and peas
gaeng plah tu-nah grapong

1 cup unsweetened coconut milk

2 to 3 tablespoons red curry paste

1 can (12 ounces) tuna, packed in oil or water, drained

¾ cup chicken broth or water

½ cup frozen peas or frozen shelled edamame beans

2 tablespoons fish sauce

2 teaspoons palm sugar or brown sugar

Keep the elements of this simple dish in your pantry and you will have the ticket to great flavor without fuss. Curry paste (any flavor), unsweetened coconut milk, fish sauce, and good-quality chunky tuna cover the curry, and a big sack of jasmine rice or another fine rice variety, or couscous, rice noodles, or angel hair pasta, will make it a meal.

In a medium saucepan over medium-high heat, bring the coconut milk to a lively boil and stir well. Reduce heat to medium and add the curry paste. Simmer gently for 3 minutes, stirring often and pressing to dissolve the paste and make a smooth sauce. Add the drained tuna, chicken broth, frozen peas, fish sauce, and palm sugar, and stir gently to mix everything well. Simmer 3 to 4 minutes more until heated through, and then transfer to a serving bowl. Serve hot or warm.

Serves 4

spicy tuna salad with chilies and lime

yum tu-nah

1 can (12 ounces) chunky tuna, packed in oil
   or water, drained

3 tablespoons fish sauce

3 tablespoons freshly squeezed lime juice

1 tablespoon sugar

2 tablespoons thinly sliced shallots

2 green onions, thinly sliced crosswise

1 tablespoon minced fresh ginger (optional)

1 tablespoon coarsely chopped roasted, salted
   peanuts (optional)

1 tablespoon finely chopped fresh hot green
   chilies, or 1 teaspoon coarsely ground
   dried red chili

2 tablespoons coarsely chopped fresh cilantro,
   plus a few extra cilantro leaves for garnish

*This belongs in your repertoire for when you are too tired to cook but still crave something delicious. I stuff it into warm pita bread, scoop it up bite by bite with crackers, and spoon it into lettuce cups for a tiny, tangy little wrap on the party table. The fresh ginger and chopped peanuts are terrific, but not essential. For a more rustic flavor, use palm sugar and stir in a dollop or two of roasted chili paste (*nahm prik pao*). For a spread-on-bread sandwich, stir in a little mayonnaise or olive oil, and top with thick tomato slices and thin, lengthwise slices of peeled cucumber.*

Combine the tuna, fish sauce, lime juice, sugar, shallots, green onions, ginger (if using), peanuts (if using), chilies, and chopped cilantro in a medium bowl. Mix gently to season the tuna and break it into smaller chunks. Transfer to a small platter or shallow bowl, garnish with cilantro leaves, and let stand 10 to 15 minutes. The salad can also be covered and chilled until shortly before serving time, up to 2 days. Serve chilled or at room temperature.

Serves 4

shrimp with snow peas
goong paht tua li-song

2 tablespoons vegetable oil

2 tablespoons chopped garlic

½ pound medium shrimp, peeled and deveined

2 cups fresh snow peas, stemmed, or 1½ cups shelled edamame beans, fresh or frozen

3 tablespoons fish sauce

2 tablespoons water or chicken broth

2 teaspoons sugar

A beautiful dish, this one, a minuet of opposites attracting and then dancing round the kitchen. Plump, moist shrimp meets flat, crisp legume, shrimp pink meets spring green, spiral meets straight line, rich flavor meets fresh sensible crunch. It is pretty, tasty, and easy. Snow peas are easy to find these days, and need only a quick snipping off of the stem end. I also love this dish with edamame beans, the neon-green fresh soybeans long popular in Japan and China. Here in North Carolina we can find them fresh and local, in farmers' markets and super-markets. Both Asian groceries and supermarkets often have them frozen as well.

❀ Heat the oil in a large skillet or a wok over medium-high heat until a bit of garlic sizzles at once. Add the garlic and toss well until fragrant. Add the shrimp and toss until they turn pink.

❀ Add the snow peas, fish sauce, water, and sugar and cook, tossing now and then, until snow peas are bright green, hot, and tender and the shrimp are cooked, 1 to 2 minutes. Transfer to a serving plate and serve hot or warm

Serves 4

shrimp with roasted chili paste and fresh basil
goong paht nahm prik pao

3 tablespoons vegetable oil

1 tablespoon chopped garlic

1 pound medium shrimp, peeled and deveined

3 tablespoons roasted chili paste (*nahm prik pao*)

2 tablespoons fish sauce

¼ cup water or chicken broth

1 teaspoon sugar

1 cup fresh Asian or Italian basil leaves or fresh mint leaves or fresh cilantro leaves (optional)

2 long red fresh *chee fah* chilies, sliced crosswise into ovals, or a small handful of long, thin strips of sweet red bell pepper (optional)

It's so simple and so good, you will soon be dreaming up other ways to enjoy this delicious stir-fried dish. Thais love this pairing of plump pink shrimp with rustic chili sauce and fresh herbs. Another classic version uses hoi lai, a delicate little clam with a thin, beige shell sporting a chocolate-colored herringbone design. In Thailand, market vendors offer "kits" to remind you how quick and easy this dish is: Dozens of tall clear-plastic sacks, each brimming with a kilo of clams topped off with a flourish of fresh basil and a red chee fah chili or two. I have made this with Manila clams, using an extra half-pound to allow for the weight of the shells. Try it with scallops, strips of beef, or chunks of chicken as well. Use fresh mint or cilantro if you do not have fresh basil, or a handful of thinly sliced green onion in lieu of mint.

❀ Heat the oil in a large, deep skillet or a wok over medium-high heat until a bit of garlic sizzles at once. Add the garlic and toss well until fragrant. Add the shrimp and toss until they turn pink.

❀ Add the roasted chili paste, fish sauce, water, and sugar, and continue cooking for 1 to 2 minutes, tossing occasionally, until shrimp are cooked through and coated with sauce. Add the basil leaves, if using, and toss well. Turn out onto a serving platter, garnish with the red chilies, if using, and serve hot or warm.

Serves 4

shrimp with lemongrass, chilies, and lime
plaa goong

2 stalks fresh lemongrass

2 tablespoons thinly sliced shallots

1 tablespoon finely chopped fresh hot green
chilies, such as Thai chilies, serranos,
or jalapeños

¾ cup fresh mint leaves, thinly sliced

¾ pound medium or large shrimp, peeled
and deveined

3 tablespoons freshly squeezed lime juice

2 tablespoon fish sauce

½ teaspoon sugar

If you like ceviche, you will love this tart, bright dish. The juxtaposition of hot green chilies with cool lime and mint makes for an herbal flavor explosion. Grilling the shrimp is standard for plaa goong, *but you can poach them as well, or use cooked shrimp left from a recent feast. The lemongrass needs to be sliced paper thin, so that its fibrous texture becomes pleasing to eat. You could also mince it very fine, or grind it to a paste with one tablespoon of the lime juice and a little water before mixing it into the sauce. If you do not have fresh lemongrass,* mai pen rai, *"never mind." You will still have a fabulous tangy pile of shrimp even if you leave it out. Serve* plaa goong *with a stack of lettuce cups from the heart of a bibb or Boston lettuce. Then tuck a shrimp or two into a lettuce leaf, making a little wrap for eating out of hand.*

❀ If grilling, prepare a very hot fire in a charcoal grill or heat a gas grill on high. If poaching, bring a medium saucepan of water to a boil over high heat.

❀ Meanwhile, trim the lemongrass stalks down to about 2 inches, including the rounded base. Trim the root end to make it smooth, and peel off any loose, brittle outer leaves. Cut remaining stubs of fragrant stalk crosswise into very thin slices, or chop them to a fine mince, about 2 tablespoons. Set aside with the shallots, chilies, and mint.

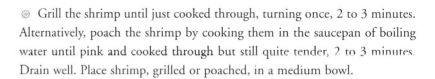 Grill the shrimp until just cooked through, turning once, 2 to 3 minutes. Alternatively, poach the shrimp by cooking them in the saucepan of boiling water until pink and cooked through but still quite tender, 2 to 3 minutes. Drain well. Place shrimp, grilled or poached, in a medium bowl.

Add the lime juice, fish sauce, and sugar and mix well. Add the lemongrass, shallots, chilies, and mint and toss well. Transfer to a serving platter and serve warm, at room temperature, or chilled.

Serves 4 to 6

rice & noodles

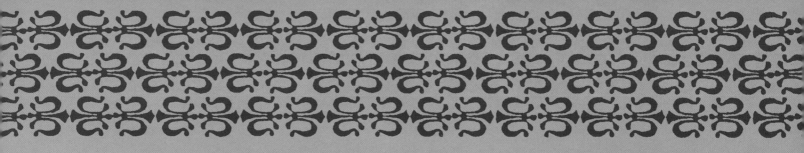

INTRODUCTION TO RICE & NOODLES

Rice is the key to the magnificent cuisine of Thailand. The myriad ingredients, captivating aromas, and intense flavors that make Thai food unique evolved from a simple ancient imperative: to make the rice go down. Thais eat rice with a pleasure and dedication that I couldn't comprehend until I had lived for several months in a small town, eating simple country food. Without butter or even salt for flavor, Thai rice seemed so plain. But as I ate rice, plate after plate, meal after meal, day after day, I came to see "plain" as a good thing, describing the simplicity of rice, its satisfying, generous essence as the bearer of good food, and as fuel for our daily life. Most Thais, in fact most of the people of Asia, prefer not to go a day without eating rice.

Thai people love a big, juicy piece of grilled chicken as much as anyone, but they eat it in pinches, pulled off and paired with bite-sized lumps of sticky rice. They adore a bowl of *mussamun* curry, studded with potatoes, peanuts, and big chunks of tender beef, but they spoon the sauce onto plain rice and enjoy the meat in small bites, appreciating what it does for the rice. In an upcountry home, one chicken fortifies a curry that will feed ten people, as long as there are lots of little side dishes and lots and lots of rice.

Then there are noodles, a Chinese import warmly welcomed to the Thai table long ago. Not all Thai noodle dishes are quick and easy, but many are, such as Soy Sauce Noodles with Beef and Greens (page 104), Rice Noodles with Lettuce and Ground Beef Gravy (page 112), and Rice Noodles in Soup with Roast Chicken and Crispy Garlic (page 114). I have also adapted several more complex noodle dishes such as Chiang Mai Curry Noodles (page 116) and Paht Thai Noodles (page 107), streamlining here and there to create a delicious version for your everyday kitchen.

sticky rice
kao niow

2 cups long-grain sticky rice

Water for soaking and steaming

This extraordinary rice is the daily bread of Laos, and consequently of northern and northeastern Thailand, where the Laotian cultural connection is so strong. Sticky rice, sometimes labeled "sweet rice" and "glutinous rice" in English and gao nep *in Vietnamese, is a long-grain variety with a natural propensity for clinging to itself in a pleasing, convenient way. You can pinch off a hunk of the rice and roll it into a chewy, bite-sized ball, yet it does not stick to your fingers or to much else that it touches. Look for it in Asian markets. Before cooking, it looks like rice grains painted a dazzling, flat shade of white. Steam changes the hard white grains into soft, plump, ivory grains that cling together delightfully with the slightest encouragement.*

Plan ahead to enjoy this great Southeast Asian treat, as it must soak in water to cover for at least three hours. Traditionally, whoever is cooking sets the breakfast rice out to soak the night before, and then leaves the supper rice soaking in the morning before heading out to school, to the office, to the rice fields. See "Useful Utensils for Cooking Thai Food" (page 146) for information on steaming devices for cooking sticky rice.

❀ Put the raw sticky rice into a medium bowl and add enough water to cover it by 2 inches. Leave it to soak for at least 3 hours and as long as overnight.

❀ To cook, set up your steaming vessel. Bring about 4 inches of water to a vigorous boil over medium heat in the base of your steamer. Drain the rice well and transfer it to the steaming basket. Secure the basket of rice above but not touching the steaming water, and let it cook in a steady flow of steam for 30 to 40 minutes, checking the water level now and then and replenishing if needed. When the rice plumps up, glistens, and changes color from bright white to translucent ivory, test it by pinching up a small mouthful, rolling it into a ball, and eating it. If it's tender and chewy, it's ready.

✺ Turn the cooked sticky rice out onto a cutting board or tray at once and spread it out into a fairly even layer to release steam and cool a bit, 3 to 4 minutes. Then gather the warm rice into a large mound and transfer to a serving plate or a *gateep,* a traditional covered serving basket. To hold it for longer than 20 minutes, cover it with a kitchen towel to help keep it moist. Serve hot, warm, or at room temperature.

Makes about 4¼ cups

jasmine rice
kao hohm mali

1½ cups jasmine rice

2 cups water

Jasmine rice is the house rice of Thailand, grown in the lush central plains and naturally endowed with a nutty, pleasing aroma that emanates from the rice pot when the rice is almost cooked. Jasmine rice smells wonderful, but nothing like the jasmine flower's exotic perfume. The name makes a little leap, associating one appealing aroma with another, despite the vast difference between their scents. I love my 10-cup rice cooker, which makes enough rice for a crowd or just a few cups when I cook for my family. But knowing how to cook a good pot of rice is a grand feeling, so here is a basic recipe. Rice almost triples in volume after cooking, so be sure your pan has room for the transformation.

Measure the rice into a medium saucepan and add cold water to cover the grains. Swirl the grains with your hand, drain well, and do the same thing two more times. Drain well, and then add the measured 2 cups of water. Bring to a gentle boil, uncovered, over medium heat. Let the rice boil gently until the water level drops below the level of the rice, so that it looks dry. Stir well, cover, and reduce heat to low. Cook 15 minutes, and then let stand, covered, 10 minutes more. Fluff gently, and then serve hot or warm.

Makes about 5 cups of rice

shrimp fried rice with pineapple
kao paht goong sapparote

4 cups cooked jasmine rice (facing page),
preferably chilled

2 tablespoons vegetable oil

1 tablespoon coarsely chopped garlic

½ cup chopped onion

½ pound medium shrimp, peeled
and deveined

2 tablespoons fish sauce

½ teaspoon sugar

1 can (8 ounces) crushed pineapple,
undrained, or 1 cup finely chopped
fresh pineapple

2 tablespoons thinly sliced green onions

What a gorgeous platter of food this makes! Line up your ingredients next to the stove, and you will find this comes together fast. Supermarkets often carry fresh pineapple peeled and ready to chop into perfect tidbits for this dish, if you want to dress it up a little. But then again, canned pineapple can be waiting for you in the pantry, for the night you need a little something special for your own sweet self.

⚜ Prepare the rice by crumbling it with your fingers, breaking up the bigger lumps, and set aside in a bowl.

⚜ Heat a wok or a large, deep skillet over high heat. Add the oil, and when a bit of garlic sizzles at once, add the garlic and onion and toss well until shiny and fragrant, about 1 minute. Add the shrimp and cook, tossing now and then, until the onion begins to wilt and the shrimp are pink and cooked through, 2 to 3 minutes.

⚜ Add the rice, fish sauce, and sugar and and toss well. Add the pineapple and green onions and cook about 2 minutes more, tossing often, until the rice is tender and heated through. Mound the rice on a serving platter and serve hot or warm.

Serves 4

thai fried rice
kao paht

4 cups cooked rice, preferably chilled

2 tablespoons vegetable oil

1 tablespoon coarsely chopped garlic

½ cup chopped onion

¼ pound boneless pork or chicken, thinly sliced into 2-inch strips

1 large egg, beaten

2 tablespoons fish sauce

1 teaspoon sugar

2 green onions, thinly sliced crosswise

A handful of fresh cilantro leaves, coarsely chopped

Accompaniments (Optional)

Cucumber slices

1 lime, quartered lengthwise

Fish sauce seasoned with chopped fresh hot chilies or ground dried red chilies

For most Thai people, making fried rice is like making a sandwich in the West: there's not much to it. Fried rice is a formula for quick and easy meals that a) take very little time and effort; b) make good use of leftovers; and c) taste like you worked harder than you did. Get in the habit of cooking more rice than you need for a particular meal, as fried rice begins with room-temperature rice; cold, hard rice from the refrigerator is even better. You can add cooked meat rather than uncooked, decreasing cooking time since it only needs reheating. I love kao paht *topped with an over-easy fried egg, making it* kao paht pi-seht: *special fried rice. I also like to add frozen peas or edamame beans as soon as the meat is cooked, and serve it with chunks of ripe tomato and a simple salad.*

❀ Prepare the rice by crumbling it with your fingers, breaking up the bigger lumps, and set aside in a bowl.

❀ Heat a wok or a large, deep skillet over high heat. Add the oil, and when a bit of garlic sizzles at once, add the garlic and onion and toss well until shiny and fragrant, about 1 minute. Add the pork and cook, tossing often, until the onion begins to wilt and the meat is cooked through, about 2 minutes. Add the beaten egg, and toss well to scramble it once it begins to set.

❀ Add the rice, fish sauce, sugar, and green onions and cook, tossing often, until the rice is tender and heated through. Mound the rice on a serving platter and garnish with the cilantro, and if desired, the cucumber slices and wedges of lime to squeeze over each serving. Accompany with small bowls of fish sauce with chopped chilies, and serve hot or warm.

Serves 4

soy sauce noodles with beef and greens
kwaytiow paht si-yu

½ pound dried rice noodles, fettucine or linguine width

3 tablespoons fish sauce

2 tablespoons dark soy sauce

1 tablespoon molasses, honey, or brown sugar

½ teaspoon salt

½ teaspoon freshly ground pepper

3 tablespoons vegetable oil

1 tablespoon coarsely chopped garlic

½ pound boneless beef, such as tri-tip, flank steak, or rib eye, thinly sliced crosswise into 2-inch strips

5 cups loosely packed fresh spinach leaves, or 4 cups collard greens cut in big bite-sized pieces, or 3 cups broccoli florets

¼ to ½ cup water or chicken broth, as needed to cook the collard greens or broccoli, if using, and the noodles

2 eggs, lightly beaten

This classic Thai lunchtime choice is traditionally made with wide, soft ribbons of fresh rice noodles called kwaytiow sen-yai. *Here in North Carolina, I use the widest dried rice noodles I can find. They look like a brittle, white cousin of fettucine, but thin ones work fine as well, and both widths soften up nicely as they soak and then cook. You can substitute 1 pound of fresh, soft rice noodles, adding them to the hot pan right after you've cooked the greens, and cooking them only 1 minute to heat through.*

Dark soy sauce and molasses give this hearty noodle dish its dark, gorgeous color and deep flavor, nicely balanced between salty and sweet. Thais use si-yu wahn, dark sweet soy sauce, a combination of the two often available in Asian markets. You can use it in this recipe if you have it on hand. Paht Thai is spicy, but paht si-yu is mild in terms of chili heat. For the playful flavor counterpoint Thais love, make prik nahm som, *the standard condiment served with* paht si-yu: *Stir a spoonful of sugar into a small bowl of white vinegar, and top it with thinly sliced fresh hot green chilies.*

❁ To prepare the dried rice noodles, bring a large saucepan of water to a rolling boil, add the noodles, and remove from heat. Let the noodles steep 5 minutes, and then drain and rinse well in cold water. Transfer the drained rice noodles to a medium bowl and place it by the stove.

❁ In a small bowl, stir together the fish sauce, soy sauce, molasses, salt, and pepper. Place it by the stove, spoon and all, along with a serving platter, a pair of long-handled tongs or a spatula, and a slotted spoon for tossing the noodles. Have all the remaining ingredients ready and handy.

❀ Heat a large, deep skillet or a wok over medium-high heat and add 2 tablespoons of the oil. Swirl to coat the surface, add the garlic, and toss for 30 seconds. Scatter in the beef and toss well. Add the spinach and cook, tossing often, until it is shiny, bright green, and tender and the beef is cooked, 1 to 2 minutes (collards and broccoli will need a splash of water and an extra minute or two of cooking). Transfer the beef and spinach to the serving platter.

❀ Reduce heat to medium, scatter in the noodles, and toss well. Cook 2 minutes or so, tossing and pulling the noodles apart so they cook evenly, and adding splashes of water as needed to keep them moist and prevent sticking. When the noodles have softened, curled up, and turned white, push them to the side of the pan.

❀ Add the remaining tablespoon of oil to the pan. Pour in the eggs and when they are almost set, toss to scramble, and mix them in with the noodles.

❀ Return the beef and spinach to the pan. Add the soy sauce–molasses mixture, using the spoon to get every sticky drop. Toss everything well for about 1 minute until the noodles are a handsome brown. Transfer to the serving platter and serve hot or warm.

Serves 2 to 4

paht thai noodles
kwaytiow paht Thai

¼ pound dried rice noodles, linguine or fettucine width

3 tablespoons vegetable oil

1 tablespoon coarsely chopped garlic

8 to 10 medium shrimp (about ¼ pound), peeled and deveined

¼ pound boneless chicken or pork, cut in bite-sized pieces

3 tablespoons fish sauce

2 tablespoons soy sauce

2 tablespoons sugar

½ teaspoon dried red chili flakes or chili powder

About ¼ cup water or chicken broth, to prevent noodles from sticking

1 egg, lightly beaten

3 green onions, coarsely chopped (about ⅓ cup)

2 cups fresh bean sprouts

¼ cup coarsely chopped dry-roasted peanuts

2 tablespoons freshly squeezed lime juice

2 lime wedges

If you love this dish as much as I do, you will be thrilled to see how easily you can make it in your home kitchen. Our daughter Isabelle has grown up calling paht Thai *"pink noodles" since her favorite version at Indra Thai restaurant, in Glendale, California, includes just enough tomato paste to give it a delicious tinge of pink. The classic noodle-shop version calls for a daunting array of ingredients, from pickled white radish and garlic chives to tamarind liquid, dried shrimp, and crisp fried tofu. My family loves this simple and delicious homestyle* paht Thai *recipe we learned from Ms. Siriluk Williams, owner of Sukothai Restaurant in Fort Lauderdale, Florida—it's easy to make and hard to resist. Cooking noodles in a wok or a skillet takes a little practice, but once you have prepared a few plates of* paht Thai, *you will know just what to do and how to do it. For the rice noodles, or* kwaytiow, *the traditional choice is a slender, flat noodle resembling linguine, but almost any long noodle will work here.*

❀ To prepare the dried rice noodles, bring a large saucepan of water to a rolling boil, add the noodles, and remove from heat. Let the noodles steep 5 minutes, and then drain and rinse well in cold water. Transfer the drained rice noodles to a medium bowl and place it by the stove, along with a serving platter, a pair of long-handled tongs or a spatula, and a slotted spoon for tossing the noodles. Have all the remaining ingredients ready and handy.

❀ In a large, deep skillet or a wok, heat 2 tablespoons of the oil over medium heat until a bit of garlic sizzles at once. Add the garlic, toss well, and then add the shrimp and chicken. Cook about 2 minutes, tossing now and then, until shrimp and meat are cooked through.

continued

❀ Add the noodles and toss as they begin to soften, whiten, and curl in the hot pan. Add the fish sauce, soy sauce, sugar, and chili flakes and cook 1 to 2 minutes, tossing now and then. Add a splash or two of the water to prevent sticking.

❀ When the noodles are tender, push them to one side and add the remaining tablespoon of oil. Add the egg, and once it is almost set, scramble it and push it aside. Add the green onions and 1 cup of the bean sprouts and cook about 1 minute, tossing once or twice, until shiny and beginning to wilt.

❀ Sprinkle the peanuts and lime juice over the noodles and then toss to mix everything well. Mound the noodles on a serving platter, arrange the remaining cup of bean sprouts and the lime wedges on the side, and serve hot.

Serves 2 to 4

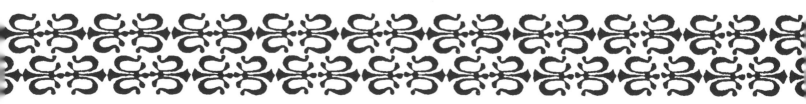

tangy bean thread noodles with cilantro and lime
yum woon sen

1 medium bundle dried bean thread noodles
(about 3½ ounces), or about 3 cups cooked
bean thread noodles

2 tablespoons vegetable oil

2 tablespoons coarsely chopped shallots

1 tablespoon coarsely chopped garlic

¼ pound ground pork, beef, chicken, or turkey

2 tablespoons fish sauce

1 teaspoon soy sauce

2 teaspoons sugar

1 teaspoon dried red chili flakes

2 tablespoons freshly squeezed lime juice

2 tablespoons thinly sliced green onions

2 tablespoons finely chopped fresh cilantro
or mint

10 to 12 Boston, bibb, or iceberg lettuce leaves

Bean thread noodles are delightful and quick cooking. Made in China and Taiwan from small round green mung beans, they often come dried into tight skeins, and packed 8 or 10 bundles to a bag. They are so hard when dry that it's difficult to cut them. Softened in water for a few minutes, they become flexible enough to cut, and with the briefest cooking in boiling water or a hot skillet, they transform into a clear, bouncy noodle that absorbs flavors well. If you can find only a large bundle, soften the whole batch, and measure out the 3 cups you need. Serve with lettuce leaves for wrapping.

❀ Bring a medium saucepan of water to a rolling boil and drop in the wiry mass of noodles. Remove from heat at once and let the noodles cook in the very hot water until they become clear and tender, no more than 1 minute. Drain, rinse with cold water and drain again. Mound noodles on your cutting board in a horizontal mass, cut crosswise into 2-inch lengths and set aside in a medium bowl. You'll have about 3 cups.

❀ In a medium frying pan or wok, heat the oil over medium heat until a bit of garlic sizzles at once. Add the shallots and garlic and cook until they are shiny and fragrant, about 1 minute. Add the meat, toss well, and then add the fish sauce and soy sauce. Stir-fry until the meat is done, another minute or two, and remove from heat. Scatter in the noodles and toss well. Return to the bowl and let cool to room temperature.

❀ Add the sugar, chili flakes, lime juice, green onions, and cilantro, and toss well. Mound on a serving platter along with the lettuce leaves and serve at room temperature.

Serves 4

muslim-style rice noodles with beef and tamarind
kwaytiow is-sa-lahm

¼ pound dried rice noodles, or ½ pound fresh rice noodles, fettucine width

¼ cup fish sauce

¼ cup tamarind liquid (page 150) or Indian-style tamarind chutney, or 2 tablespoons white vinegar mixed with 1 tablespoon soy sauce and 1 tablespoon sugar

2 tablespoons sugar

1 tablespoon dark soy sauce or soy sauce

1 tablespoon molasses, honey, or brown sugar

3 tablespoons coarsely chopped shallots

2 teaspoons coarsely ground dried red chili flakes

½ cup water

½ cup unsweetened coconut milk

½ pound boneless beef, such as tri-tip or flank steak, thinly sliced crosswise into 2-inch strips

2 cups bite-size pieces Chinese broccoli or big bite-size pieces of collard greens or spinach leaves

I learned this fabulous noodle dish from Ms. Nongkran Daks, cooking teacher, author of Thai Noodles and Snacks, *and chef-owner of the acclaimed Thai Basil Restaurant, near Dulles Airport in Chantilly, Virginia. In this unusual southern-Thai specialty, coconut milk mellows the sweet-tart edge of tamarind, and the deep rich flavor and color of dark soy sauce play off the vivid green of Chinese broccoli. You could use fresh soft rice noodles cut into big fat ribbons if you have them, but rest assured that the fettucine-width dried rice noodles carried by most Asian groceries will give you an exceptional dish. Store-bought Indian-style tamarind chutney makes an excellent shortcut for tamarind liquid in this dish.*

❀ Place the dried rice noodles in a medium bowl with enough warm water to cover them. Soak until the noodles are bright white, softened, and flexible, but still too tough to eat, about 15 minutes. Drain well and place the noodles by the stove.

❀ Meanwhile, in a medium bowl stir together the fish sauce, tamarind liquid, sugar, dark soy sauce, and molasses, and place by the stove, spoon and all. Combine the shallots, chili flakes, and ¼ cup of the water in a small food processor or a blender. Grind to a thick paste and place it by the stove.

❀ In a large, deep skillet or a wok over medium heat, combine the remaining ¼ cup water with the coconut milk and bring to a gentle boil. Stir in the shallot-chili paste and and cook 1 to 2 minutes, until fragrant and thickened.

⚜ Scatter in the beef, toss well, and then add the Chinese broccoli. (If you use spinach, stir it in just before transferring the noodles to the serving platter.) Cook for a minute or two, tossing now and then, until the beef changes color and the Chinese broccoli turns a vivid, shiny green.

⚜ Add the noodles and cook 1 minute, stirring to coat them with the sauce. Give the fish sauce mixture a good stir and then scrape the mixture into the pan. Stir well and cook, tossing gently now and then, until the noodles are tender and the sauce is smooth, 1 to 2 minutes. Transfer to a serving platter and serve hot.

Serves 4

rice noodles with lettuce and ground beef gravy
kwaytiow neua sahp

¾ pound dried rice noodles, fettucine or linguine width

5 large leaves of lettuce, or 3 to 4 cups mixed salad greens

5 roma (plum) tomatoes, or 12 cherry tomatoes

3 tablespoons vegetable oil

1 tablespoon dark soy sauce or soy sauce

2 to 3 tablespoons water, as needed to keep noodles from sticking

1 tablespoon coarsely chopped garlic

¾ pound ground beef

2 tablespoons fish sauce

1 teaspoon curry powder

1 teaspoon sugar

1½ cups chicken broth or water

2 tablespoons cornstarch or flour, dissolved in 3 tablespoons water

¼ cup coarsely chopped fresh cilantro

During my years in Thailand, the Peace Corps headquarters in Bangkok was located at the end of Soi Somprasong 2, a meandering urban lane off Petchaburi Road. About halfway down was a pleasant open-air noodle cafe where my friends Sandi, Dudley, Mary Claire, and I often stopped for a satisfying plate of kway-tiow neua sahp. *Since the sauce is a simple gravy made with ground beef, it is a particularly quick and easy noodle dish to make at home. I like to serve the noodles on leaves of bibb, Boston, or oak leaf lettuce, or a plate of shredded iceberg lettuce. Serve it with an over-easy fried egg on top, if you want the Soi Somprasong #2 special version.*

❀ To prepare the dried rice noodles, bring a large saucepan of water to a rolling boil, add the noodles, and remove from heat. Let the noodles steep 5 minutes, and then drain and rinse well in cold water. Transfer the drained rice noodles to a medium bowl and place it by the stove.

❀ Line a serving platter with the lettuce leaves. Stem and quarter plum tomatoes or halve cherry tomatoes, mound on platter to one side, and place platter by stove.

❀ In a large, deep skillet or a wok, heat 2 tablespoons of the vegetable oil over medium heat and add the rice noodles. Toss and stir the noodles, and add the soy sauce when they begin to curl, shine, and turn from ivory to bright white. Cook 2 to 3 minutes more, tossing and stirring often, until the noodles are tender. Add a few tablespoons of water as needed to keep them cooking without sticking. Pile the hot noodles on the lettuce-lined serving platter and set aside.

✳ Add the remaining tablespoon of vegetable oil to the pan along with the garlic and cook 1 minute over medium-high heat. Crumble in the ground beef and stir well as it begins to brown. Stir in the fish sauce, curry powder, sugar, and chicken broth and let the sauce come to a boil.

✳ Stir the cornstarch mixture well and then scrape it into the skillet. Cook, tossing often, until the sauce thickens, about 2 minutes more. Pour the meat sauce over the warm noodles, sprinkle with the cilantro, and serve hot.

Serves 4

rice noodles in soup with roast chicken and crispy garlic
kwaytiow nahm gai

½ pound dried rice noodles, linguine width

¼ cup vegetable oil

3 heaping tablespoons coarsely
  chopped garlic

5 cups chicken broth

About 2 cups very coarsely chopped roast
  chicken or Chinese-style roast duck, or
  thinly sliced Chinese-style barbecued pork

¼ cup fish sauce

1 teaspoon freshly ground pepper

3 green onions, thinly sliced crosswise

A handful of fresh cilantro, coarsely chopped

In Thailand you can enjoy tender noodles around every corner, in great big bowls brimming with delicious broth. Market vendors and noodle cafes serve customers from before dawn until well past midnight. Some traveling noodle-mongers bring the entire operation to their customers, charcoal stove and all, in twin baskets bobbing from a length of bamboo balanced on their shoulders. Since noodles literally come to them, Thais don't make soup noodles at home, but they could, and so can you.

This is a get-you-started recipe, intended to acquaint you with the basics of soup noodle dishes. Then you are off, on your way to making the easiest Asian fast food as confidently and casually as you assemble a sandwich. To expand your repertoire, use cooked shrimp or meatballs instead of roast chicken, cooked Chinese-style egg noodles, angel hair pasta, or elbow macaroni instead of the rice noodles, and chopped peanuts instead of crispy garlic for crunch. Add bean sprouts for a cool note or choppped chilies for heat—you will be amazed how delicious and varied this simple dish can be.

Thais seldom use chopsticks, but for noodles they make an exception, especially when it is noodles in soup. You can offer your guests both chopsticks and forks for the noodles and big spoons for the soup, so that they can enjoy their noodles down to the last slurp.

❀ Bring a large pot of water to a lively boil and remove from heat. Drop in the dried rice noodles and let stand 8 to 10 minutes, stirring now and then to separate the noodles as they cook. When noodles are tender enough to eat but still firm, drain, rinse with cold water, drain well, and set aside.

❀ Meanwhile, place a small heatproof bowl by the stove and heat the oil in a small skillet over medium heat for 1 minute. Add the garlic and cook, stirring now and then, until it becomes fragrant and golden but not brown, about 2 minutes. Pour garlic and oil into the bowl and set aside.

❀ Bring the chicken broth to a gentle boil in a large saucepan over medium heat, and then add the chicken, fish sauce, and pepper. Simmer 1 to 2 minutes, until the meat is heated through. Remove from heat.

❀ To serve, set out four big soup bowls and divide the noodles among them. Top each serving of noodles with an equal portion of the garlic, oil and all. Ladle 1¼ cups of hot broth and chicken over the noodles in each bowl, sprinkle each serving with green onions and cilantro, and serve hot.

Serves 4

chiang mai curry noodles
kao soi

2 tablespoons vegetable oil

1 tablespoon finely chopped garlic

2 tablespoons red curry paste or *panaeng* curry paste

¾ pound boneless chicken, cut in big, bite-size chunks, or boneless beef, such as tri-tip or flank steak, thinly sliced crosswise into 2-inch strips

2 cups unsweetened coconut milk

1¾ cups chicken broth

2 teaspoons ground turmeric or curry powder

2 tablespoons dark soy sauce or soy sauce

1 teaspoon sugar

1 teaspoon salt

2 tablespoons freshly squeezed lime juice

1 pound fresh Chinese-style egg noodles, or ½ pound dried Chinese-style egg noodles, angel hair pasta, or spaghetti

⅓ cup coarsely chopped shallots

⅓ cup coarsely chopped fresh cilantro

⅓ cup thinly sliced green onions

In northern Thailand, kao soi *is a meal for one, served up in an enormous bowl and garnished with a playful tangle of crunchy egg noodles, fried crisp for a contrast in texture to the tender noodles and smooth, sunny-colored sauce. The standard condiments include Chinese-style ground chilies in oil, chopped pickled cabbage, and wedges of lime. To make crispy noodle nests, you'll need about ½ pound thin fresh egg noodles. Heat about 2 cups vegetable oil in a wok or small deep skillet to about 375 degrees F. Carefully add a handful of noodles, let it sizzle and brown a few seconds, turn gently with tongs, and transfer the "nest" to a platter to cool. Serve in individual soup bowls with chopsticks or forks for the noodles, and big spoons for the delicious curry sauce.*

❀ Heat the vegetable oil in a medium saucepan over medium heat, and then add the garlic. Toss well and add the red curry paste, mashing and stirring to soften it in the oil, about 1 minute. Add the chicken and cook 1 to 2 minutes, tossing now and then to brown it evenly and mix it with the curry paste. Add the coconut milk, chicken broth, turmeric, soy sauce, sugar, and salt and stir well. Bring to a gentle boil and adjust heat to maintain a lively simmer. Cook about 10 minutes, until meat is cooked through. Stir in lime juice, remove from heat, and cover to keep curry warm while you prepare the noodles.

❀ Cook the noodles in a large pot of rapidly boiling water, until tender but still firm, as little as 2 minutes for fresh noodles and 7 minutes or more for dried. Drain, rinse well in cold water, drain again, and divide the noodles among individual serving bowls. Ladle on hot curry, and sprinkle each serving with the shallots, cilantro, and green onions. Serve hot.

Serves 4 to 6

vegetables, salads, a pickle & a sauce

INTRODUCTION TO VEGETABLES, SALADS, A PICKLE & A SAUCE

Please do not tell the good people of Thailand that vegetables are good for them. They have no idea. The only reason they eat their vegetables is because they like them. They like the way vegetables taste and the way they look. They like the way vegetables crunch and exude coolness when raw, the way they soften and shine when put to the flame.

They like lettuce and raw cabbage leaves as edible spoons: They use them to scoop up bites of chili-flecked salads and then eat the whole bundle with sticky rice. They like bean sprouts in a steaming bowl of noodles at the early morning market. They chomp on raw green beans and they pop cherry tomatoes like, well, popcorn.

They eat cucumbers all the time, with fried rice, with peanut sauce, with yellow curry, and with *nahm prik* chili sauces. And as if all that were not enough, they hollow them out, stuff them with ground pork, and cook them in a delicate soup. Thais do not know that cabbage is to be boiled for ages, served up, and then ignored—they cook cabbage and its cruciferous vegetable cousins with garlic just until bright green and wilted enough to be chewed without an audible crunch. Then they eat it, lots and lots of it, with rice.

So please do not tell Thai people that vegetables are good for them; that good food and vegetables should live in different countries, separated by mountains too steep to climb. Let them keep eating their vegetables with pleasure and with abandon, all the time, every which way, five times a day. I suppose it won't hurt anyone.

green papaya salad
som tum

1 tablespoon coarsely chopped garlic

1 tablespoon dried shrimp (optional)

1 to 2 teaspoons coarsely chopped fresh hot green chilies, such as Thai chilies, serranos, or jalapeños

1½ cups shredded green papaya, or 1 cup shredded cabbage plus ½ cup shredded carrots

12 green beans or 3 Asian yard-long beans, trimmed to 1-inch lengths

2 tablespoons fish sauce

1 tablespoon freshly squeezed lime juice

2 teaspoons palm sugar or sugar

6 to 8 cherry tomatoes, halved

2 tablespoons coarsely chopped roasted, salted peanuts

All over the Thai kingdom, this cool, sharp, spicy, crunchy, and crazy salad has folks lined up, waiting patiently for the som tum *vendor. Stiff shreds of unripe papaya, wilted in a mortar by blows from a sturdy pestle and dressed with an essence of fish sauce, lime juice, tomatoes, and sugar, goes with sticky rice, with garlicky grilled chicken, with anything* Issahn, *and with nothing but a spoon. Composed salads have their place, but give me* som tum, *that pungent little haystack of Thai flavor explosion. If you do not have a mighty mortar and pestle, do not despair. I have suggested one easy way to subdue the shreds and work in the seasonings, and you may think of more. You can serve* som tum *on the side like cole slaw, or with lettuce cups or small leaves for scooping it up and eating it out of hand.*

To prepare using a mortar and pestle, combine the garlic, dried shrimp (if using), and chilies in a large, heavy mortar and use the pestle to pound and grind them to a very coarse paste. Add the papaya and green beans, pounding, scraping, and turning with a spoon now and then, for 1 to 2 minutes, until the papaya shreds are wilting and seasoned and beans are somewhat smashed.

If you do not have a large mortar and pestle, use a rolling pin. Mince the garlic and chilies and place them in a medium bowl along with the dried shrimp. Spread the papaya out on your cutting board, and light into it with the rolling pin for a minute or two, pressing down hard, and mowing back and forth. Stop to gather up the shreds, squeeze them, and spread them out again for another pass or two. When the shreds are wilted, transfer them to the bowl. Repeat with the green beans, pressing down just until they split open and wilt a bit, and then add them to the bowl.

continued

✿ Add the fish sauce, lime juice, and palm sugar to the papaya and use the pestle to press and grind the mixture a little, and a spoon to turn and mix everything well. Or use your hands to squeeze the mixture a few times and work in the seasonings.

✿ Add the cherry tomatoes and peanuts, toss well, and then mound the salad on a small serving platter, juices and all. Serve at room temperature.

Serves 4

spinach with black pepper and garlic
pahk spi-naht paht gratiem prik thai

2 tablespoons vegetable oil

1 tablespoon coarsely chopped garlic

8 to 10 cups loosely packed fresh spinach leaves (about 20 ounces)

2 tablespoons fish sauce

2 teaspoons sugar

½ teaspoon black pepper

¼ cup water

Here is your template for cooking both leafy greens and stemmy greens, quickly and deliciously. This is a streamlined pahk boong fai daeng, *the classic stir-fry of a slender, hollow-stemmed vegetable known as* pahk boong *in Thai and as* ung choy, kang kong, *water spinach, and morning glory, among other names.*

A wok is handy for corralling the potential avalanche of raw spinach leaves before the heat shrinks them down to a plateful, but a large, deep skillet will work. Having two long-handled utensils handy helps you toss and turn the greens. Try making this with napa cabbage, rapini, savoy cabbage, and baby bok choy. For broccoli, peel stems, slice them crosswise into coins, and cook with the florets. For bok choy, chop white stems into 2-inch lengths and cook them first, adding the green leafy portion after they are tender.

❀ Heat the oil in a large heavy skillet or a wok over medium-high heat for about 1 minute, and then add the garlic. Toss well and then add the spinach. Gently turn the pile of spinach to heat most of the leaves and add the fish sauce, sugar, pepper, and water. Toss well, and then cook, turning often, until the spinach is wilted and tender, 1 to 2 minutes. Turn out onto a deep platter, sauce and all, and serve hot, warm, or at room temperature.

Serves 4

pink grapefruit salad with toasted coconut and fresh mint
yum some-oh

3 tablespoons shredded coconut

2 tablespoons freshly squeezed lime juice

2 tablespoons fish sauce

1 tablespoon sugar

2 cups bite-sized chunks peeled, sectioned
pomelo or grapefruit

2 tablespoons dried shrimp, coarsely chopped,
or 2 tablespoons coarsely chopped roasted,
salted peanuts (optional)

1 tablespoon coarsely chopped shallots

2 teaspoons finely chopped fresh hot
green chilies or dried red chili flakes

½ cup coarsely chopped fresh mint or cilantro

Leaves of Boston lettuce or bibb lettuce
for accompaniment

If you like Thai food for its bright flavors, you will find this dish positively dazzling. Thais make it with pomelo, grapefruit's thick-skinned, misshapen, and sweeter cousin. Pomelo is quite dry, and fairly easy to pull apart by hand. To prepare this salad using the juicier grapefruit, use two forks to gently tease grapefruit sections into smaller chunks. Look for unsweetened shredded coconut in natural-food stores, or buy the sweetened shredded coconut available in the supermarket baking section. A little extra sweetness is welcome, and the sugar makes the coconut brown beautifully and fast. To prepare yum some-oh *ahead of time, hold the toasted coconut and dried shrimp or peanuts aside until just before serving time, so that they will keep their crunch. Serve with spoons and small lettuce leaf cups for wrapping around the salad and enjoying bite by bite.*

❀ Toast the shredded coconut in a small, dry skillet over medium-high heat for 3 to 4 minutes, tossing often, until most of it turns a rich, soft brown. Turn out onto a saucer to cool.

❀ In a medium bowl, combine the lime juice, fish sauce, and sugar and stir well to dissolve sugar and form a smooth sauce. Add the pomelo, toasted coconut, dried shrimp (if using), shallots, chilies, and mint, and toss gently to combine everything well. Transfer to a serving platter with lettuce leaves on the side, and serve at room temperature.

Serves 4

roasted eggplant salad with cilantro and lime
yum makeua yao

1 pound Asian or globe eggplant

2 tablespoons thinly sliced shallots

2 tablespoons coarsely chopped fresh cilantro, plus leaves for garnish

2 green onions, thinly sliced

2 teaspoons coarsely chopped garlic

3 tablespoons fish sauce

3 tablespoons freshly squeezed lime juice

1 tablespoon sugar

1 tablespoon chopped fresh hot green chilies, or 2 teaspoons coarsely ground dried red chilies

1 tablespoon dried shrimp, whole or coarsely chopped, or 2 tablespoons coarsely chopped roasted, salted peanuts (optional)

The long, slender Asian varieties of eggplant are ideal for this dish, but a plump globe eggplant will do. This dish is wildly popular all over Southeast Asia, sometimes including pork and fresh shrimp. This is my simple version, often on our supper table since dark purple Asian eggplant adore life in my summer garden, and thrive until the most strident frost has its way. Our only problem is deciding whether to use them in a curry or in this terrific salad. Serve it with lettuce cups or leaves for scooping up into handy little wraps, or as part of a meal with rice.

✿ If you use long, slender Asian eggplant, cut them in half lengthwise. If you use a globe eggplant, cut it lengthwise into quarters. Cook these eggplant strips, skin-side down, on a lightly oiled hot grill until tender and lightly browned, or on a baking sheet in a 400-degree F oven for about 15 minutes. Set aside to cool.

✿ Meanwhile, place all of the remaining ingredients in a medium bowl. Cut the thick strips of eggplant crosswise into 2-inch chunks and add to the bowl. (If you use globe eggplant, peel the strips first.) Gently toss well to mix the eggplant with the seasonings. Mound the salad on a small platter, juice and all, and garnish it with a pinch of fresh cilantro leaves. Serve at room temperature or chilled.

Serves 4

three-flavor relish with dried shrimp, chilies, and lime
yum goong haeng

½ cup dried shrimp

¼ cup freshly squeezed lime juice

2 tablespoons fish sauce

2 tablespoons sugar

2 tablespoons thinly sliced shallots

2 teaspoons minced fresh hot green chilies

I learned this recipe from Ms. Krissanee Ruangkritya, chef-owner of Siam Orchid Restaurant in Orlando, Florida, and author of Adventures in Thai Food and Culture. *The flavor dance of Thai cuisine is wonderfully on display in this simple condiment: saltiness from fish sauce and dried shrimp; heat from fresh hot green chilies; sweetness from sugar; and a bright, tart edge from freshly squeezed lime juice. I serve this as I would a chutney or salsa with a simple meal of jasmine rice with curry, peas, or cucumber slices, and Easy Omelet with Sri Rachaa Sauce (page 59).*

❀ Soak the dried shrimp in warm water to cover for 5 minutes, and then drain well. Chop them coarsely and put them in a small bowl.

❀ Add the lime juice, fish sauce, sugar, shallots, and chilies and stir well. Serve at room temperature with rice and other dishes. Or cover and refrigerate for a day or two.

Serves 4 to 6

tangy cucumber pickles
ah-jaht

½ cup white vinegar

½ cup water

½ cup sugar

1 teaspoon salt

1 large hothouse cucumber or 6 small garden cucumbers (about 1 pound)

3 tablespoons thinly sliced shallots or coarsely chopped purple onion

2 teaspoons thinly sliced fresh hot red chilies or finely chopped fresh hot green chilies

Cucumbers are a mainstay of Thai cooking, sliced and placed at the base of steaming servings of fried rice, hollowed out and stuffed with seasoned pork for a clear soup, and seasoned with a sweet and tangy brine for this delicious, ubiquitous little pickle. This humble relish is standard issue with Chicken Satay with Spicy Peanut Sauce (page 24), Spicy Fish Cakes with Green Beans and Wild Lime Leaves (page 15), Yellow Curry Chicken with Potatoes (page 42), and Chicken Hidden in Curried Rice (page 54). Also called taeng kwa dong, *the relish is made with short, plump summer garden cucumbers, but hothouse cucumbers make an excellent version as well. If you use the big, dark green, grocery-store cucumbers, do this first: peel well, halve lengthwise, scoop out seeds with a spoon, and then slice crosswise into sturdy little crescents. Except when serving it with satay, Thais often crown this refreshing salad with a tablespoon of chopped peanuts and 2 tablespoons of chopped fresh cilantro.*

※ In a medium saucepan, combine the vinegar, water, sugar, and salt. Cook over medium heat, stirring often, until the sugar and salt dissolve, 3 to 4 minutes. Remove from heat and let the dressing cool to room temperature.

※ Peel cucumbers and cut them lengthwise into 4 long strips. Slice each strip crosswise into small triangles. (You should have about 3 cups.) Place in a small serving bowl or divide among several small serving bowls. Top with the chopped shallots and chilies. Shortly before serving, pour the cooled dressing over the cucumbers. Serve at room temperature or cover and refrigerate for a day or two, and serve cold.

Makes about 2 cups

sweet-hot garlic sauce
nahm jeem gratiem

1 cup sugar

½ cup white vinegar

½ cup water

2 tablespoons coarsely chopped garlic

1 teaspoon salt

1 tablespoon chili-garlic sauce (*sambal oelek*), or Sri Rachaa sauce, or minced fresh hot red chili peppers, or 1 to 2 teaspoons dried red chili flakes

Sweet-Hot Garlic Sauce is simply wonderful and wonderfully simple. Heat transforms six humble ingredients into a beautiful red-gold sauce, a perfect foil for crisp fried spring rolls and the garlicky richness of gai yahng, *Grilled Garlic Chicken, Issahn Style (page 57). To give this sauce its spicy edge, you have many options. My favorite is chili-garlic sauce (*sambal oelck*). This fire-engine red purée of fresh hot red chilies, garlic, and vinegar has visible seeds and a serious kick, and gives the best color. Other good choices are Sri Rachaa sauce; Tabasco sauce; dried red chili flakes; or a generous spoonful of minced and mashed fresh hot red chilies. Many Asian markets carry a decent version of this dipping sauce.*

Sweet-Hot Garlic Sauce makes a pleasing accompaniment to Sticky Rice (page 98), and anything grilled or fried; on the other hand, it tastes delicious tossed with steamed asparagus or broccoli, mixed with mayonnaise, or splashed into dressings and dips. I try to keep it on hand all the time. My dear friend and fellow cookbook author Crescent Dragonwagon likes it so much, she includes it in her magnum opus, The Passionate Vegetarian, *with a new name: Thai Crystal.*

In a medium saucepan, bring the sugar, vinegar, water, garlic, and salt to a gentle boil over medium heat, stirring well to dissolve the sugar. Simmer 8 to 10 minutes, until you have a thin, smooth syrup. Remove from heat, stir in chili-garlic sauce, and set aside to cool. (If you use fresh hot red chili peppers or dried red chili flakes, use a fork to mash them up on your cutting board with the garlic and the salt, and then scoop the coarse paste into the warm sauce.) Serve at room temperature with Grilled Garlic Chicken, Issahn Style (page 57), or any other grilled or crisp-fried food. Sealed in a glass jar, it keeps in the refrigerator for up to 1 week.

Makes about 1¼ cups

sweets & drinks

INTRODUCTION TO SWEETS & DRINKS

Here are a few sweet little gems, in tribute to the love of sweet things I found in the land of smiles. You may have read that a traditional Thai meal does not include a dessert course in a Western sense. This is not because Thais do not cherish sweets, but because they enjoy them throughout the day. Thais see no reason to wait until the end of a proper dinner to indulge in sweet pleasures. They snack on sweet things from dawn until well past my bedtime, tucked in between plates of rice and bowls of noodles. Why try to pack in a piece of pie and coffee after a meat-and-potatoes meal? It is inspired, like the custom of tea in the United Kingdom.

Nun Bananas in Coconut Milk (page 135) is the kind of warm, comforting dish that can be breakfast or a midnight snack, especially if you make it in wintertime with the kabocha pumpkin variation. Sticky Rice with Mangoes (page 136) is justifiably world famous, for its juxtaposition of textures, flavors, and colors is brilliant. It is reason enough to learn to cook sticky rice. Coconut Ice Cream (page 141) is glorious, and takes all of ten minutes for the preparation phase. Little countertop ice-cream makers have become more affordable of late, so consider splurging on one. If you like ice cream as much as I do, it would be a sweet little investment in your quick and easy kitchen.

thai iced tea
cha yen

4½ cups water

¾ cup Thai tea powder

¾ cup sugar

Crushed ice or ice cubes to fill each glass

1 to 1½ cups evaporated milk or half-and-half
 (3 to 4 tablespoons per glass)

Thai Iced Tea makes me think of my sister Susanne, who upon entering her local Thai restaurant, orders her first tall tumbler of Thai tea as she walks to her table. Maybe frequent enjoyment of this beautiful, scrumptious drink is the reason she herself is so sweet.

Sold in one pound cellophane-wrapped packets in Asian markets, this finely chopped black tea is spiced with cinnamon, star anise, and vanilla, and then tinged with a bit of food coloring to create its gorgeous terra-cotta hue. Like Thai coffee, Thai tea is traditionally sweetened well with sugar as it brews and crowned with a generous splash of evaporated milk or half-and-half just before serving. You can brew Thai tea in a teapot, drip coffeemaker, or French press, making it very strong and adding the sugar while the tea is still very hot.

In a medium saucepan over medium heat, bring the water to a boil, stir in the Thai tea powder, and remove from heat. Stir well to mix in the sugar and then let it cool, stirring occasionally to dissolve sugar.

When the tea has cooled to room temperature, strain it through a fine-mesh strainer or coffee filter into a pitcher and chill until serving time. To serve, fill 4 to 6 tall glasses with ice and then add about ¾ cup Thai tea to each glass. Top off each glass with 3 to 4 tablespoons evaporated milk. Serve at once, as the evaporated milk cascades over the ice and swirls languidly into the tea.

Serves 4 to 6

thai iced coffee
kah-feh yen

4½ cups water

¾ cup Thai coffee powder

¾ cup sugar

Crushed ice or ice cubes to fill each glass

1 to 1½ cups evaporated milk or half-and-half
  (3 to 4 tablespoons per glass)

Look for Thai coffee powder in one-pound cellophane-wrapped packages in Asian markets. Its peculiar but pleasing flavor comes from roasted corn and roasted sesame seeds. Thai iced coffee is served sweetened with sugar and topped off with a luxurious layer of evaporated milk or half-and-half. If you want your iced coffee black, leave off the creamy flourish and you have kah-feh dahm yen, also known by its Chinese name, o-liang. You can brew Thai coffee in a drip coffee-maker or a French press, making it extra strong and stirring in the sugar while the coffee is still hot.

❀ In a medium saucepan over medium heat, bring the water to a boil and then stir in the Thai coffee powder. As soon as the mixture returns to a boil, remove the pan from heat, stir in the sugar, and let it cool, stirring occasionally to dissolve sugar.

❀ When the coffee is cool, strain it through a fine-mesh strainer or a coffee filter into a pitcher and chill until serving time. To serve, fill 4 to 6 tall glasses with ice and then add about ¾ cup Thai coffee to each glass. Top off each glass with 3 to 4 tablespoons evaporated milk. Serve at once, as the evaporated milk cascades over the ice and swirls into the coffee.

Serves 4 to 6

nun bananas in coconut milk
gluay buat chee

3 to 4 medium bananas (about 1½ pounds),
   preferably a bit underripe

1 cup unsweetened coconut milk

1 cup water

½ cup sugar

½ teaspoon salt

In Thailand, Buddhist monks wear robes the color of pumpkin, but Buddhist nuns wear robes as white as freshly grated coconut. This homey snack of banana chunks "enrobed" in a sauce of warm sweet coconut milk goes by the whimsical name of gluay buat chee, *or "bananas ordained as nuns."*

Thai soil nourishes numerous varieties of bananas, some considered ideal for fritters, others for stewing with sticky rice for banana leaf–wrapped puddings, and still others for preserving in sugar syrup. This dish is traditionally made with gluay nahm wah, *a short, sturdy banana variety. The bananas in your supermarket, known in Thailand as the "fragrant banana" or* gluay hohm, *will be wonderful here, as will many of the exotic bananas available from specialty produce purveyors.*

I freeze any leftovers, and whirl them in the blender with ice cubes and fresh or frozen fruit for a breakfast shake. You can also make this with peeled kabocha pumpkin or another sturdy winter squash, using about 3½ cups of bite-sized pieces, replacing half the sugar with palm sugar or brown sugar, and simmering 5 to 10 minutes, until the pumpkin is tender.

❀ Peel the bananas and halve lengthwise. Cut each half crosswise into about 4 equal pieces, giving you about 2½ cups of banana chunks.

❀ Bring the coconut milk, water, sugar, and salt to a gentle boil in a medium saucepan over medium heat. Stir well to dissolve the sugar, and then add the bananas. Simmer gently for 1 to 2 minutes. Remove from heat and ladle into small bowls. Serve hot or warm.

Serves 4 to 6

sticky rice with mangoes
kao niow mamuang

1½ cups long-grain sticky rice, soaked in
   water to cover 3 hours or overnight

2 cups unsweetened coconut milk

1 cup sugar

2 teaspoons salt

6 ripe, sweet mangoes

A lovely thing about being in Thailand during the sweltering heat of mango sea-son is that, when it is too hot to cook, you can stroll down to the night market and have sticky rice and mangoes for supper. In fact, the kitchen heat generated in cook-ing this glorious dish is minimal, and the results are sweet compensation indeed. Even if you do not have special equipment for steaming food, you can cook the amount of sticky rice needed for this heavenly sweet treat using a stockpot or Dutch oven as a makeshift steamer. See "Useful Utensils for Cooking Thai Food" (page 146) for detailed information on steamers.

Once you have mixed in the coconut sauce, this luscious rice is best eaten within a few hours. If you have some left, cover and chill for a day or two, and then reheat gently in a microwave or a steamer. If you can't find ripe mangoes, use about 1½ cups per person of another ripe, sweet fruit, such as sliced fresh peaches or strawberries, or a mixture of blueberries, raspberries, and bananas, tossed with a little sugar, a squeeze of lime, and a sprig of mint.

Drain the soaked sticky rice and transfer it to a steamer basket. Place the steamer basket over several inches of water in a saucepan or the base of a steamer. Bring the water to a rolling boil over medium-high heat. Cover and cook, adjusting the heat to maintain a steady flow of steam, until the rice swells and glistens and is sticky enough to pinch into pleasing chewy lumps, 30 to 45 minutes. Replenish the steamer base with boiling water as needed to maintain the flow of steam.

continued

❀ While the rice is steaming, combine the coconut milk, sugar, and salt in a medium saucepan over medium heat. Cook and stir gently for 3 to 4 minutes, until the sugar and salt dissolves into a smooth sauce. Remove from heat and set aside.

❀ When the rice is cooked, transfer it to a large bowl; you will have about 4 cups cooked sticky rice. Pour the sweetened coconut milk over the rice and stir gently to mix it evenly into the hot rice. Cover, and set aside for at least 30 minutes and as long as 3 hours, to let the rice absorb the sauce. Meanwhile, peel the mangoes and cut the flesh off the long flat pits. Cut it into generous chunks and set aside.

❀ To serve, place a fist-sized portion of coconut rice and an equal portion of the mango chunks on each of 6 salad or dessert plates. Serve at room temperature with a fork and spoon.

Serves 6

sweet potato pudding maw gaeng
kanome maw gaeng

Custard

3 large eggs

1 cup unsweetened coconut milk

1¼ cups palm sugar or sugar

1¼ cups cooked and mashed sweet potatoes

Crispy Shallots (optional)

3 tablespoons vegetable oil

2 tablespoons thinly sliced shallots

My wonderful sister Linda fell in love with this sweet treat at Indra, her neighborhood Thai restaurant in Glendale, California. Two small pans were perfect divvied amongst our happy family entourage. Maw gaeng *is the specialty of Petchaburi, the sweets capital of Thailand, located en route to Hua Hin and other seaside destinations along the Gulf of Siam. There it is made with mung bean centers or taro root, but sweet potato, acorn squash, and butternut squash also make delicious versions. I love the strange traditional finish of crispy shallots, but with or without them,* maw gaeng *is a treat.*

⊛ Heat oven to 400 degrees F and lightly grease an 8- or 9-inch square baking pan. To prepare the custard: In a medium saucepan, stir together the eggs and the coconut milk and then mix in the palm sugar. Add the sweet potatoes and stir well. Bring to a gentle boil over medium heat, stirring often, until the sugar dissolves and the custard thickens a bit, 4 to 5 minutes.

⊛ Pour the custard into the prepared pan and bake for 30 to 40 minutes, until puffed and golden brown; a butter knife inserted in the center should come out clean.

⊛ To prepare the crispy shallots: Heat the oil in a small skillet over medium-high heat. When a bit of shallot sizzles at once, scatter in the shallots and fry until golden brown and crisp, 3 to 5 minutes. Scoop out shallots and about 1 tablespoon of their oil and transfer to a saucer to cool. Sprinkle them over the warm custard and then let it cool. Serve at room temperature, cut into small squares to eat with a fork or spoon.

Makes about 16 small squares

coconut ice cream
ai-teem ga-ti

**7 cups unsweetened coconut milk
(about four 14-ounce cans)**

2 cups sugar

1 teaspoon salt

Luxuriously sweet and rich, coconut ice cream tastes wonderful and takes only minutes to make. Simply halve the recipe for a small ice-cream maker. You can prepare the coconut ice-cream mixture in advance and then keep it, covered and chilled, for up to 1 day before churning it. If you want your coconut ice cream to go, you could assemble the little ice-cream sandwiches I enjoyed in the night market in the northern town of Chiang Rai: Place two small, very firm scoops of coconut ice cream on a piece of white bread. Add a small portion of Sticky Rice (page 98) and a sprinkling of chopped peanuts, fold the bread up around the goodies, and enjoy.

Combine the coconut milk, sugar, and salt in a medium saucepan and bring to a gentle boil over medium-high heat. Cook, stirring often, until the sugar dissolves and the mixture is smooth, 1 to 2 minutes. Transfer to a bowl, cool to room temperature, and then cover and chill until very cold. Transfer to the bowl of an ice cream maker and freeze according to manufacturer's directions. Serve at once, or transfer to an airtight container and freeze for up to 2 weeks.

Makes about 1½ quarts; serves 8 to 10

MENUS FOR QUICK & EASY THAI MEALS

✸ Breakfast Special

Thai Fried Rice (page 102), with crisp bacon replacing the pork

Pink Grapefruit Salad with Toasted Coconut and Fresh Mint (page 124)

Thai Iced Coffee (page 134), served hot with sweetened condensed milk

✸ Ready-When-You-Are Luncheon

Chicken-Coconut Soup (page 28)

Jasmine Rice (page 100)

crisp green salad with crushed pineapple, cherry tomatoes, and toasted pumpkin seeds

lemon and raspberry sorbets with ginger cookies

✸ School Lunch

Spicy Tuna Salad with Chilies and Lime (page 90) served with shredded lettuce in pita bread

rice cakes with chunky peanut butter

chunks of fresh ripe honeydew, mango, or apple

✸ Your Kids Will Love It

Shrimp Fried Rice with Pineapple (page 101), with peas replacing shrimp

Easy Omelet with Sri Rachaa Sauce (page 59)

lemonade

Nun Bananas in Coconut Milk (page 135)

✸ My First Very Quick and Very Easy Thai Meal

Yellow Curry Chicken with Potatoes (page 42)

Easy Omelet with Sri Rachaa Sauce (page 59)

sliced cucumbers and tomatoes

Jasmine Rice (page 100)

three kinds of ice cream and cookies

✸ Winter Feast for Ten

Mussamun Curry Beef with Potatoes and Peanuts (page 45)

Tangy Cucumber Pickles (page 128)

Jasmine Rice (page 100)

green salad with toasted walnuts and diced pears

warm apple crisp with vanilla ice cream

✿ Summer Feast for Ten

Chicken Satay with Spicy Peanut Sauce (page 24)

toast triangles for dipping in spicy peanut sauce

Tangy Cucumber Pickles (page 128)

potato salad with green onions, peas, and fresh mint

Thai Iced Tea (page 133)

Coconut Ice Cream (page 141) with lemon cookies

✿ A Flavorful Picnic

Soft Spring Rolls with Shrimp and Fresh Mint
(page 17)

tomato sandwiches with mayonnaise, salt,
and pepper

deviled eggs with minced green onions and cilantro

peanut butter cookies

✿ Almost Too Hot to Cook

Issahn-Style Minced Pork Salad with Crunchy Rice
and Fresh Mint (page 77)

couscous with chopped cilantro, tomatoes, and
tiny peas

vanilla ice cream with fresh strawberries, bananas,
and peaches

✿ On the Grill

Grilled Salmon with Chili-Lime Sauce (page 86)

Crying Tiger Steak with Roasted Tomato–Chili
Sauce (page 71)

grilled eggplant, asparagus, peppers, and zucchini

couscous tossed with chopped green onions and
toasted pine nuts

✿ A Tailgate Party

Crispy Pork Spareribs with Black Pepper and Garlic
(page 23)

Grilled Beef Salad with Chilies and Lime (page 74)

sliced cucumbers and carrot sticks

Spicy Peanut Sauce (page 24) tossed with angel
hair pasta

tortilla chips and spicy salsa

blondies and fudge brownies

❀ **Beach House Blast**

lots and lots of shrimp boiled in the shell

Sweet-Hot Garlic Sauce (page 129) and spicy cocktail sauce

Crispy Omelet with Oysters and Bean Sprouts (page 60) with Sri Rachaa Sauce

waldorf salad

Coconut Ice Cream (page 141) with fried bananas and toasted walnuts

❀ **You Make Thai Soups, They Bring Great Bread and Desserts**

Meatball Soup with Spinach and Crispy Garlic (page 29)

Chicken-Coconut Soup (page 28)

Shrimp and Lemongrass Soup (page 30)

delicious breads

wonderful desserts

❀ **A Northern Thai Menu**

Northern-Style Dipping Sauce with Ground Pork and Tomatoes (page 22)

Sticky Rice (page 98)

sliced cucumbers and cabbage wedges

Chiang Mai Curry Noodles (page 116)

chunks of fresh pineapple and watermelon

❀ **A Southern Thai Menu**

Catfish Fillets Fried with Turmeric, Southern Style (page 82)

Chicken Hidden in Curried Rice (page 54)

Tangy Cucumber Pickles (page 128)

❀ **A Northeastern Thai Menu**

Grilled Garlic Chicken, Issahn Style (page 57)

Green Papaya Salad (page 121)

grilled hot and garlicky sausages with peanuts and slices of cucumber and fresh ginger

beef jerky with Sri Rachaa Sauce

cabbage wedges, cucumbers, and trimmed green beans

Sticky Rice (page 98)

❁ Night Market

Spicy Cashew Salad with Chilies, Cilantro, and Lime
(page 19)

Paht Thai Noodles (page 107)

Coconut Ice Cream (page 141) with Sticky Rice
(page 98) and chopped peanuts

❁ Get Well Soon!

Rice Soup with Chicken, Cilantro, and Crispy Garlic
(page 33)

baked sweet potato with butter, brown sugar,
and cinnamon

hot green tea with honey

❁ Soup and Sandwich

Roasted Eggplant Salad with Cilantro and Lime
(page 126)

sliced tomatoes and cucumbers

warm pita bread

blue corn chips with hot salsa

cream of tomato soup

Thai Iced Tea (page 133)

USEFUL UTENSILS FOR COOKING THAI FOOD

Blenders, Small Food Processors, Mortar and Pestle

For turning fresh herbs into flavorful seasoning pastes, you can use a blender or a small-capacity food processor. You will usually need to pause and scrape down the sides during the process, and to add water to get the blades moving so that everything gets ground together smoothly and well. Since Thai recipes often call for small amounts of very fibrous ingredients, such as lemongrass, ginger, and galanga, you need a small, deep workbowl that keeps everything contained and in close proximity to the whirling blades. If you would like to use a traditional heavy Thai mortar and pestle, or *kroke,* for these jobs, look among the cookware in an Asian grocery store. The squat, bluish black stone *kroke* is made entirely of granite. Ranging in size from tiny to huge, this *kroke* pulverizes lemongrass fibers and whole spices into seasoning pastes with ease. A big one is ideal, but small ones are fine if you work in batches as needed. The tall, rustic Lao-style *kroke* is glazed ceramic or clay with a sturdy wooden pestle. It makes short work of *som tum,* or Green Papaya Salad (page 121), with its large, deep bowl. Both kinds are objects of beauty as well as service, worthy of a place on your kitchen counter when not in use.

Coffee Grinders for Whole Spices, Dried Shrimp, and Peanuts

Small electric coffee grinders do a grand job of reducing spices and other tiny, hard, tough, and dry foods to a powder, coarse or fine. They turn dry-fried grains of rice into deliciously gritty and aromatic roasted rice powder for northeastern Thai salads. You can also use them to grind a small quantity of peppercorns for a countertop supply in a flash; grind peanuts for satay sauce, *panaeng* curry, or *paht Thai;* or grind dried shrimp to a delicate powder. Pulse your coffee grinder on and off if you need a coarse, gritty texture, but for fine powder, just let it rip. You can't get by with one grinder if you love freshly ground coffee, as even fans of flavored coffees blanch at the thought of dried prawn tidbits in their cups of joe. Dedicate one grinder for coffee, and use the other for everything else.

Devices for Steaming Food

In most Asian kitchens, steaming is a basic, everyday cooking process, but in the West it presents a challenge. Asian markets and mail-order sources often carry traditional steaming equipment, and you can improvise a steamer as well. For steaming Sticky Rice (page 98), look for a Laotian-style two-piece steamer, a simple cone-shaped woven basket and a deep lightweight pot. The basket holding soaked and drained sticky rice fits into the pot, suspending the rice over several inches of steaming water. It is perfect for the job, widely available, and cheap. For steaming a variety of foods including sticky rice, look for big Chinese-style steamers made of lightweight metal and consisting of a stack of perforated trays fitted over a wide base. In addition to these two complete steamer sets, you can find both simple wire racks and handsome stacked sets of bamboo trays, both of which fit into a wok, resting snugly halfway down the sides over several inches of steaming water. For bamboo tray sets, bigger is better since they can hold more food per steaming session. You can improvise a steamer using a pasta pot with an insert, or a stockpot or big Dutch oven with an empty tuna can turned steaming ring. For the pasta pot, bring several inches of water to a boil in the pot, place a bowl or plate of food on the perforated insert, and lower the insert into the pot for steaming. For the stockpot or Dutch oven, remove the bottom lid and label from an empty tuna can, leaving a thick ring. Place this steaming ring on the bottom of the stockpot and add an inch or so of water, so that the top of the ring pokes out above the water level. Balance a plate, pie pan, or shallow bowl of food on the steaming ring, bring the water to a boil, cover, and steam until the food is cooked.

Electric Rice Cookers

This masterpiece of electrical ingenuity completely simplifies the cooking of rice, that quintessential task at the heart of Thai cuisine. You measure the rice into the pot, rinse, swish, and drain it well, and then add the proper amount of water, easily measured on the side of the pot. Then press a button and you are free—free to chop, free to fry, free to call your beloved sister in Seattle and chat until you hear a graceful "ping." This sound means that perfectly delicious rice awaits you. How does it know? Magic, surely, very good magic. Get a big one,

5 to 10 cups, because it will also make a diminutive 2 to 3 cups should you so desire, as well as a party-sized batch when you want that. I like to cook too much rice for a given meal, as it reheats so nicely and can easily become fried rice or rice soup.

Kitchen Scissors

Two Thai cooking tasks justify the time and money required to buy some good kitchen scissors. Snipping hanks of softened bean thread noodles into manageable two-inch lengths is one job, and cutting wild lime leaves crosswise into infinitesimal threads is the other. Sure, you don't do either of those jobs on a daily basis, but perhaps that's because you have not done them with a pair of kitchen scissors dedicated to culinary tasks. Look in kitchen equipment stores and hardware stores for a heavy pair that is dishwasher safe, and then keep it both in and for the kitchen, resisting any urges to carry it off to the den for wrapping birthday presents. Once you have a pair, you will find many other kitchen uses for them.

Knives

Good knives will serve you well almost every time you cook Thai food. You need a well-made paring knife and either a big Chinese cleaver or a 10-inch chef's knife. I have one of each, which is unnecessary but useful when I need a clean blade in the middle of cooking a dish. You also need several sturdy cutting boards. I like to keep one for meat and fish and two for vegetables and herbs, to avoid cross-contamination between meats and other foods. The classic Thai cutting board is a cross-section of a tamarind tree, thick, round, and plump, like a miniature wheel of *Parmigiano-Reggiano*. Heavy cutting boards work best, and all of them stay put if you place a damp kitchen towel on your countertop and place the cutting board on top of the towel.

Noodle Bowls and Saucers for, Well, Sauces

While you are in an Asian market picking out a mighty cleaver or choosing between *panaeng* curry paste and *mussamun* curry paste, check out the housewares shelves, where you will often find an array of porcelain and plastic serving pieces, large and small. Consider buying a few of the big, deep and wide bowls designed for individual servings of noodles in broth or instant ramen, and a supply of the tiny saucers and small shallow bowls designed to hold individual portions of dipping sauces and condiments. These are useful not only for serving and eating but also for measuring out prepared ingredients to place by the stove at the ready for a stir-fry.

Pots and Pans

The wok is basic to a traditional Thai kitchen, but while I love my big, heavy carbon-steel wok I do most of my cooking in a large, deep, black cast-iron skillet. It heats up fast, holds heat well, handles large quantities of food, and is designed for a flat-top Western-style stove. Most Thai cooks upcountry use their woks on small bucket-shaped charcoal stoves or on propane burners designed to accommodate a wok's rounded shape. A good electric wok works well for the majority of Thai dishes, including curries and stir-fries, which need strong, steady heat rather than intense prolonged high heat. Though it takes up counter space, it frees your stove for other simmering pots, and the solid, balanced base keeps it steady while you scoop and stir. Any large, deep skillet will serve you well, along with a small skillet and a few saucepans. A big Dutch oven with a tight-fitting lid helps if you want to improvise a small steamer or make curry for a crowd.

Spatulas, Spoons, and Tongs for Stir-Frying

To help you cook in a swift and nimble manner, a sturdy metal or heavy plastic spatula and a slotted spoon work very well. The spatula helps you turn over large quantities of food quickly, and the slotted spoon lets you scoop foods like crispy shallots out of hot oil before they burn. When you cook noodle dishes, keep one tool in each hand to help you keep the noodles moving. Even better for this job is a set of V-shaped, spring-mounted stainless steel tongs, one long and the other very long. They come in handy for serving as well as cooking.

TECHNIQUES

Dry-Frying for Rustic Roasted Aroma and Taste

Thai cooks often toast whole spices and other ingredients in a dry wok or skillet, to deepen flavor, enhance texture, and release fragrance. Most common are dry-frying shrimp paste prior to using it in the fiery and pungent dipping sauces called *nahm prik,* and toasting whole coriander and cumin seeds before grinding them into curry pastes. Thai cooks also toast shreds of grated coconut for use in piquant salads and snacks, and peanuts and sesame seeds to enhance finished dishes. Dry-roasted ingredients abound in northeastern Thai cooking. Roasted dried red chilies stoke the fire in many classic *Issahn* dishes, and the rustic crunch and satisfying edgy flavor of roasted rice powder are hallmarks of a well-made *yum neua,* or grilled beef salad, and of *lahp,* or minced pork or beef with chilies and fresh mint. Use medium-high heat, and shake the pan often as you toast long-grain rice or a flurry of coconut shreds in a small skillet, using your eyes and nose to judge when you have the warm brown color and appealing aroma you seek. Turn dry-fried ingredients out onto a plate to cool before grinding.

Making Tamarind Liquid

To extract the delicious sweet and tangy essence of this dark brown fruit, pull a lump of tamarind pulp from a block of minimally processed tamarind, imported from Thailand in cellophane-wrapped 3-inch blocks and often labeled "wet tamarind." You can also use the flesh of ripe tamarind pods, available seasonally in Asian, Mexican, and Caribbean markets and many supermarket produce sections. I prefer the block, since I can keep it handy on my pantry shelf, like raisins, for months. I like to make up a batch once a week so that I can reach for it as easily as fish sauce or sugar, but you can also make up only what you need as you cook.

To make tamarind liquid, measure out about ⅓ cup of tamarind pulp from a block, or ½ cup pulp from peeled, ripe tamarind pods. Place in a small bowl with 1 cup of warm water, and let it soften, squeezing and mashing it now and then to help it dissolve. Hands are best but a big spoon will also work. After 15 minutes or so, pour the contents of the bowl through a fine-mesh strainer, and then work the remaining goo against the strainer with the back of a big spoon, pressing it onto the mesh to separate the rich brown tamarind purée from the assorted seeds, hulls, and twigs. Coax out what you can in a minute's time, about 1 cup, scraping the outside of the strainer to catch all the good stuff, and then discard what is left behind in the strainer. Transfer the tamarind liquid to a jar and refrigerate for up to 1 week. It sharpens with time, so taste it right away to get a baseline flavor. Then you can add sugar by the teaspoon to bring back the sweet-tart balance as needed after a few days.

The standard Thai substitute for tamarind is an equal amount of white vinegar or freshly squeezed lime juice. This lacks the sweetness and depth but gives the desired tang. I find Indian-style tamarind chutney, a prepared condiment available in Asian markets and many supermarkets, a very good substitute for tamarind liquid. Its standard seasonings of cumin and chilies are so common in Thai cooking that they blend beautifully with Thai dishes. I often substitute the following as well: Stir together equal parts of vinegar or freshly squeezed lime juice, sugar, and soy sauce, say 1 tablespoon of each to replace 3 tablespoons of tamarind liquid. This makes for sweet and tangy flavor and rich color, to be used at once in a given recipe.

Stir-Frying

Stir-frying is a compound word, and both words count. Note that while you can stir like crazy when that action is called for, the frying part is a job to be handled entirely by the stove, the pan, and the food. Scoop, turn, toss, and stir a bit, but then let the frying take place while you watch. If you are working all the time, you are working too hard. Wait your turn. Stir and let fry, stir and let fry. Stir only for a reason: to mix in, turn over, increase browning, prevent burning, whatever the food needs you to do.

Using Aroma and Color as Culinary Clues

Thais pay attention to smells, both as a sensual pleasure and as vital information for the cook. Aromas matter, from the scent of jasmine garlands and incense at the temple to the inviting fragrance of fresh basil and cilantro tossed onto a bowl of curry or noodles in soup. In the cuisine of Thailand and its Southeast Asian neighbors, numerous ingredients, including lemongrass, galanga, wild lime leaves, and garlic, serve an aromatic function as well as a flavoring one. Cultivate your olfactory awareness as you cook Thai food. Take note of the satisfying scent of sizzling garlic, the sweet essence of coconut milk after it simmers a bit, the brassy aroma of curry paste when it surrenders its raw edge to the persuasive heat of oil or coconut cream. It's pleasing and it gives you hints on what to do next.

Using Dried Rice Noodles

When using dried rice noodles, the standard method is to soften them first in a bowl of warm water until they change from brittle off-white strips to flexible, leathery, bright white ribbons. In this state they have become a close cousin to fresh pasta, needing a little more cooking but not the vigorous boiling you would give dried spaghetti from a box. From this state you could sauté them in oil and seasonings until they become curly, tender, and ready to eat. You could also cook them in a large pot of boiling water, unsalted, working them with tongs or a pair of long-handled spoons to keep them from clinging together in intractable gooey lumps. This will take around 5 minutes of vigilance, with frequent checking after 3 minutes to see when they reach that curly, tender state of being ready to eat. Then drain, rinse quickly in cold water, and set aside. If you don't need them at once, you can toss them in a little garlic fried in oil, or set aside and then plunge them into boiling water for a few seconds just before serving, to warm and soften them as noodle vendors do. Why not plunge the dried bundle into boiling water, like spaghetti? You can, if you take great care to tease the strands apart as they soften, and keep the separated noodles moving during the first minutes; when given the slightest chance they will gang up on you and fuse into a useless blob.

What I like to do, since I am easily and often distracted from the keen culinary focus in which I once took pride by my beloved daughters, the telephone, or a particularly compelling piece on NPR, is to bring a large pot of water to a rolling boil, remove it from the heat, and drop in the brittle mass of noodles at once, and this means without pause. I then set a loud and annoying timer for 5 minutes if I plan to stir-fry the drained noodles in, for example, *paht Thai*, or for 10 minutes if I plan to eat them with no further cooking, say, in broth or tossed with a delicious simple sauce.

Working with Chilies

Thais love chilies, and like most people around the world who enjoy cooking and eating spicy-hot food, they do not consider them dangerous. They treat them with great respect and care, as they do sharp knives and hot stoves. Just as Western cooks learn early on to use hot pads to fetch a cake pan from the oven and to hold their fingers out of the way when using a sharp knife, people in chili-loving places learn to handle chilies with care. They use their bare hands when buying, cutting, chopping, grinding, and roasting fresh and dried chilies. No rubber or plastic gloves in sight. I use my bare hands to handle chilies, and I try very hard to avoid touching my eyes when I have recently done so, as I do not like the wild burning feeling I get when I forget this important kitchen rule. But just as I still, after all these years in the kitchen, burn myself while handling a hot cookie sheet or nick my finger with a knife, I occasionally do touch my eyes with chili fingers. It hurts a lot, and I don't like it one bit. Then it stops burning, and I get back to cooking. Naturally, anyone with allergies or strong sensitivity to chilies should take great precautions, but for most of us, the thing to do is to make sensible chili-handling part of our culinary knowledge.

A THAI PANTRY

basil

Thais use leaves and sprigs of fresh basil as finishing touches on curries and soups. Most popular throughout Southeast Asia is *bai horapah (Ocimum basilicum)*, with reddish purple stems and flowers and slender, shiny, pointed leaves. Often labeled "Thai basil" and sometimes "sweet basil" and "cinnamon basil," it is bright and pungent with notes of licorice. Italian basil is a good substitute. More delicate and quite rare in the West is *bai graprao (Ocimum sanctum)*. Because this plant has deep spiritual significance within the Hindu religious tradition, it is known in English as "holy basil."

Its leaves are dull rather than glossy, with delicately serrated edges and tiny greenish flowers that protrude over the leaves like tiny grapes on stems. Thais stir-fry it with garlic, chilies, and coarsely chopped pork, chicken, or beef and relish its intense, peppery flavor in soups and in country-style curries. If you find it fresh, use it quickly, as its flavor fades quickly after harvest. Fresh mint, dill, and any other fresh basil are decent substitutes. Avoid dried basil, as it resembles its fresh self in name only. Look for holy basil seeds in Asian markets and through specialty herb growers, and try growing it in your garden.

chilies

Both fresh hot green chilies and dried red chilies provide heat to many Thai dishes. You can find *prik kii noo*, the tiny, slender, and pointed fresh Thai chili, in most Asian markets. The green ones ripen from orange to red, so a given batch will have a few harvest-colored pods amongst the green ones. Though they pack a bit less heat, fresh green serrano and jalapeño chilies make good substitutes for very hot Thai chilies. Another fresh chili you may encounter is *prik chee fah*, slender and pointed like *prik kii noo*, but larger overall and about finger length. Milder than tiny Thai chilies, these are often used as garnish. For dried red chilies, look for small incendiary ones and large, leathery ones, darker in color and milder in heat. For small ones I buy *chiles de arbol* and *chiles japones*, easy to find among Mexican ingredients in the grocery store, and for large ones I use the big, soft dark-colored chilies, about 5 inches long and often labeled "California," "New Mexico," or "Anaheim" chilies. Due to the differences in size among various chilies, I have usually called for measured amounts of chopped chilies, to simplify substituting one variety of chili for another.

cilantro

Also known as fresh coriander and Chinese parsley, cilantro is an essential ingredient in Mexican cooking, and therefore widely available in the West. Thais adore cilantro, or *pahk chee*, for its flavor, aroma, and beauty, and they toss it into spicy salads, dipping sauces, and steaming soups just before serving. A flourish of whole cilantro leaves garnishes many dishes.

cilantro roots

Outside Southeast Asia, cilantro roots have no culinary use, so the plants are often sold with the roots trimmed away. Thai cooks know their value, and mash the roots, called *rahk pahk chee*, into an aromatic and flavor-packed seasoning paste with garlic and peppercorns to start most curry pastes and to season many marinades, sauces, and stir-fried dishes. Use the slender white root along with the first inch or so of stem growing out of it, or substitute an equal amount of coarsely chopped cilantro stems and leaves. If cilantro roots are difficult to find and you do come across a batch, rinse and dry them well, double-wrap them tightly in foil or plastic wrap, and freeze for several months. Use straight from the freezer, without thawing.

coconut milk

Coconut milk provides cooks in tropical climates the luxury of making creamy sauces, soups, and sweets without benefit of grass-chomping dairy cows to provide the basic ingredient. Made by squeezing water through the finely grated white meat scraped from inside the shells of mature coconuts, coconut milk is rich and delicious, whether it is heated up with chili-fired curry pastes; simmered with pumpkin and palm sugar; or perfumed with citrusy galanga, lemongrass, and wild lime leaves in Chicken-Coconut Soup (page 28). Look for unsweetened coconut milk in cans, often in supermarkets these days. Some Asian markets carry frozen coconut milk as well. It is the nature of coconut milk to separate into an extremely thick, bright white, and even butter-solid portion, and a thin, watery, and translucent portion. This is fine, as long as it has a pleasant, almost sweet aroma. To use canned coconut milk in the recipes in this book, open a can, stir the contents together into a smooth liquid if it has separated, measure out the amount of coconut milk called for, and start cooking.

curry pastes

The curry pastes of Thailand are convenience foods with character. Pounded to a smooth, pungent paste from an array of herbs and spices, they are cooked in coconut milk or oil to release their flavor and perfume, and then simmered in coconut milk or broth with meat, fish, or seafood and vegetables until they create an extraordinary sauce sparkling with the essence of chilies, garlic, roasted cumin, whole peppercorns, wild lime zest, lemongrass, and galanga, to name only the major players. Pounding up such a *kru-eng gaeng*, which can be translated as "engine of flavor," takes time and energy beyond the scope of this book, but the commercially available curry pastes imported from Thailand provide an outstanding shortcut to the fantastic flavors of Thai-style curries. There are red curry pastes and green curry pastes, *mussamun* and *panaeng*, *lueang*, *kua,* and *kah-ree*. Each has its unique properties, but keep in mind that you can substitute freely, red for yellow and green for *gaeng kua*, without a second thought. That is except for remembering to cook rice or bring out something satisfying with which to enjoy the curry's flavors: noodles, pasta, couscous, quinoa, potatoes, or bread. I have included one recipe for a simple red curry paste (page 39), in case you cannot find a commercial source quickly, or simply want to try your hand at making it yourself.

curry powder

Curry powder, or *pong kah-ree*, is the same spice mixture sitting on your supermarket shelf and a standard minor seasoning in Thailand and throughout Southeast Asia. It probably infused its way into Thai kitchens as a Chinese culinary influence, along with five-spice powder, oyster sauce, and the family of soy sauces. Its star turn is in a Cantonese-style stir-fry of Dungeness-type crab with curry powder, fresh ginger, green onions, and egg, and in versions of fried rice. Unless labeled otherwise, most curry powder sold in Western supermarkets and those imported from Thailand are mild rather than chili-hot. Check your Asian market for an array of curry powders, including hot curry powders imported from Singapore and India.

dark soy sauce

This seasoning sauce of Chinese origin is a staple in the Thai kitchen, where *si-yu dahm* is valued as much for its color and depth as for its salty flavoring. Though it is thicker than ordinary soy sauce, dark soy sauce has a heavy but less sharp flavor. Regular soy sauce is a decent substitute. Thais also use a particular type of dark soy sauce known as *si-yu wahn*, or dark sweet soy sauce. Since it is used rarely, I have called for a substitution of dark soy sauce plus

molasses, in a ratio of 2 to 1. This means that 3 tablespoons of dark sweet soy sauce would be equal to 2 tablespoons of dark soy sauce plus 1 tablespoon molasses.

dried shrimp

Thais adore *prik haeng*, tiny flavor-packed crustaceans, for their over-the-top salty flavor, chewy texture, warm color, and cute spiral shape. Boiled, salted, and sun-dried, this shelf-stable food from the sea provides protein, texture, and flavor to mild soups; feisty *yum* such as roasted eggplant salad and green papaya salad; and the original version of *paht Thai*. Most Asian markets keep them refrigerated, and you should too, transferring them from their flat cellophane pack to a sealed glass jar. They should be bright pinkish orange with a mild oceanic scent, and they keep for about 1 month. You may find ground dried shrimp in sealed glass jars; refrigerate these in their original jars after opening as well. I love dried shrimp and hope you will too, but they can be omitted from any recipe in this book.

fish sauce

Fish sauce, or *nahm plah*, is the essence of Thai food, the bold, salty foundation on which its extraordinary flavors are built. Made from salted anchovies, this clear brown sauce looks like whiskey or iced tea and comes in long, tall glass bottles in Asian markets, and small glass and plastic bottles in many supermarkets. Neighboring Southeast Asian countries depend on it as well, both as an inexpensive source of protein and vitamin B and for its lusty flavor both in cooking and as a table condiment. Small saucers of *prik nahm plah*, minced fresh hot chilies floating in fish sauce, often accompany the enormous steaming bowl of rice that is the heart of the Thai meal. Vegetarians can omit fish sauce and simply salt the finished dish to taste. Fish sauce keeps well indefinitely at room temperature.

five-spice powder

Thais use five-spice powder, known as *pong pa-loh*, in several hearty dishes with clear Chinese roots. Mixtures vary a bit but usually include star anise, fennel seeds, Szechuan peppercorns, cloves, and cassia, a type of cinnamon. The classic five-spice dish is *kai pa-loh*, a sweet-and-salty stew of pork and hard-boiled eggs in a fragrant, coffee-colored broth (page 65).

galanga

This first cousin of ginger is known as *kha* in Thai, and in assorted languages and recipes as *languas*, *laos*, *lengkual*, *mtdaeng*, *rieng*, galangal, galingale, Java root, Siamese ginger, and Thai ginger. I am thrilled that such an exotic and incomparably delicious source of flavor and aroma is so easily found, fresh, frozen, and dried, in the West. Galanga is showcased in the extraordinary and delicious Thai soup known as *tome kha gai* (page 28). It plays a major role in Thailand's standard curry pastes, in other herb-laced soups such as *tome yum*, and in many regional dipping sauces, for which it is often roasted with garlic, shallots, and chilies to heighten its flavor and perfume. To a cook's delight, galanga is widely available in several useful forms. More Asian markets now carry it fresh. Look for knobby chunks of hard, shiny tuber, usually a delicate ivory encircled with thin dark concentric rings, but also in shades ranging to a light reddish brown. Refrigerated, it will last for weeks, loosely wrapped, preferably in plastic and in front, where you will remember to use it.

I am delighted with the frozen galanga I find in my local Asian groceries, both whole chunks and vacuum-sealed slices, imported from Thailand. The slices thaw before I get home, but this is perfect for spreading them out on a cookie sheet or plate, freezing them hard, and then gathering the individual slices into a resealable plastic bag or jar, which goes back into the freezer. Pull out a handful of slices whenever you need them and use straight from the freezer.

Still another option is whole slices of dried galanga. These big, rough woody chips may not look like the key to extraordinary and glorious Asian flavors, but they are just that. Like ginger, when galanga dries, its flavor intensifies rather than evaporates. Drop dried slices whole into soups and stews, and if you need to use them in a paste, break them into small pieces and grind to powder in a spice grinder. You could also soak them in cool water just until they are pliable, and then cut them into small grindable pieces.

If you find galanga powder in the Asian market, leave it there. As soon as dried galanga is ground to a powder the flavor and aroma fade away fast, leaving you with faintly aromatic dust. If you can't find fresh, frozen, or dried pieces, you can substitute fresh ginger—the flavor is not the same but it will make a delicious, bright-tasting, and fragrant variation.

jasmine rice

This naturally aromatic long-grain rice grows in abundance in the verdant patchwork of paddy fields that blanket Thailand's central plains. Its inviting, nutty aroma bears no resemblance to the sweet perfume of jasmine blossoms, but like jasmine flowers, this rice is precious and fragrant, a small everyday delight. Buy a big sack at an Asian market, as it keeps perfectly for many months. Other types of fragrant rice include basmati, from the foothills of the Himalayas, and an array of aromatic grains grown in Arkansas, Louisiana, and Texas. Good rice costs a bit more, but so do good chocolate and good bread, items equally worthy of a small splurge.

lemongrass

Thai cooks love the lemony taste and aroma of fresh lemongrass, using it often in delicate soups and salads and as a basic ingredient in curry paste. These days it is widely available in Asian markets and showing up more often in supermarkets as well. Unlike the flavor and aroma of ginger and galanga, the flavor and perfume of lemongrass start to fade soon after harvest. This means that, like dried mint and parsley, dried and powdered lemongrass have nothing to give us. Omit lemongrass if you cannot find it fresh or frozen, and simply season the dish until it tastes good using lime juice, fresh ginger, sugar, and salt. When you find good fresh lemongrass, preserve a supply of stalks for another day, trimming down to about 6 inches per stalk including the rounded base, wrapping the lot well in two layers of plastic wrap or aluminum foil, and freezing for up to 3 months. Use straight from the freezer, adding an extra stalk or two to boost the flavor.

long beans, or yard-long beans

Imagine a string bean snaking its way on out to a length of 18 inches or more, becoming bluish green, sweet, and so flexible you could tie it into a knot. Then you have a good idea what to expect from *tua fahk yao*, the variety of green beans common in Thailand. They taste great raw and are often enjoyed that way, cut in finger-length rods and served as a crunchy foil for spicy salads and *Issahn*-style dips. Fresh green beans make a fine substitute, but do try long beans if you find them in the marketplace.

oyster sauce

This Chinese pantry essential is standard in Thai kitchens, prized for its intense, salty flavor, its velvety texture, and the handsome brown color it provides to food. Thais call it *nahmahn hoi*, and use it in mildly seasoned stir-fries and sauces. I like it drizzled on steamed or blanched broccoli, rapini, brussels sprouts, bok choy, and *gai-lahn* (Chinese broccoli) or tossed with hot noodles, green onions, and peas.

palm sugar

Boiled down from the sap of either the palmyra palm or the coconut palm, palm sugar and coconut sugar come to market in Thailand in huge tins called *beep*, earning both these sugars the name *nahm tahn beep*.

Interchangeable in recipes, they are used to sweeten or simply for balance and complexity in the seasoning of many savory Thai dishes. Brown sugar is typical in the North, where sugarcane thrives and palm trees are scarce, and white granulated sugar is a staple in every kitchen and on noodle shop tables. Either makes a decent substitute for palm sugar. Palm sugar's texture and color vary from a lusciously thick, pale, and shiny paste resembling solidified honey, to hard, plump little cakes that can be broken up and chopped or crushed down to a powdery, measurable state. If it hardens in the jar, microwave gently to soften it.

pepper, freshly ground

Thai people had been heating up their cooking with peppercorns for centuries before the chili pepper appeared on the culinary horizon. Portuguese traders brought them from the West only a few years after Columbus got lost. Over time the fiery pod ascended the throne of Thai seasonings, but the peppercorn, *prik Thai*, still plays a subtle but significant role in modern Thai cooking. The centuries-old combination of black or white peppercorns pounded with cilantro roots and garlic into a pungent paste is the starting point of many Thai dishes to this day. Freshly ground pepper is worth a little effort. I whirl up ¼-cup batches in my spice grinder, and keep it in a sealed jar on my counter, so it is easy to scoop out as I cook.

rice flour

Made from ground jasmine rice or sticky rice, this flour is mixed into a thin batter with tapioca flour to form an appealing, chewy, noodle-like pancake in the street-food favorite, Crispy Omelet with Oysters and Bean Sprouts (page 60). You can use a combination of equal parts all-purpose flour and cornstarch in place of rice flour and tapioca flour if need be.

rice noodles

A supply of dried rice noodles should live on your pantry shelf, right between the box of spaghetti and the jar of ready-to-eat tomato sauce or the can of Italian plum tomatoes. Known throughout Southeast Asia by the Chinese name *kwaytiow*, these noodles keep for months on end. When soaked in water or cooked, they transform from pale, brittle sticks seemingly made of plastic into soft, bright white noodles, silken, satisfying, and ready for innumerable delicious preparations.

roasted chili paste

Sometimes called "chili jam" and "tome yum sauce" in Western recipes, the Thai name for this terrific condiment is *nahm prik pao*. Garlic, shallots, and small dried red chilies are roasted over a charcoal fire, pounded to a rust colored paste, and then fried in oil until dark, smooth, and loaded with fiercely delicious flavor. At this point tamarind, palm sugar, salt, and ground dried shrimp are often mixed in, transforming it into a table condiment as well as a cooking ingredient. In its commercial form these seasonings will have been added. Roasted chili paste goes into stir-fries, sauces, *tome yum,* and other soups; homemade versions are very spicy-hot. The oil may separate as it stands; just stir it back in before measuring out what you need. The English label on one widely available Thai brand reads "chilies in soya bean oil." I love *nahm prik pao* tossed with hot rice, spread on toast, or stirred into salad dressings, soups, and dips. Covered and refrigerated, it keeps well for many weeks.

Sri Rachaa sauce

Named for the seaside town on the Gulf of Siam where it originated, this crimson purée of dried red chilies, garlic, vinegar, and sugar is a simple, superb way to add chili heat. Thais use it mostly as a seasoning sauce on the side with egg dishes like Easy Omelet, or *kai jiow* (page 59). The wider world has taken to it with gusto just as Thais took to the underappreciated chili pepper when it arrived in Siam from the West centuries ago. You'll find versions of it on the table in Chinese and Vietnamese noodle parlors and Mexican taco stands, and on many grocery store shelves.

sticky rice

This unique variety of rice contains an unusual balance of the starches present in all rice, causing it to cook up to a pleasing sticky texture. Easy to pinch up into a bite-sized lump for dipping in sauces and scooping up food, it is satisfying and simply fun to eat. Fortunately, it sticks mostly to itself but not to fingers, clothes, or cooking utensils. *Kao niow* is the daily bread of Laos and consequently of northern and northeastern Thailand, where Lao cultural influence is strong. Look for long-grain rice, extremely white in color and often labeled as "sweet rice" or "glutinous rice." Use only sticky rice imported from Thailand or Laos, and plan to soak it at least 3 hours and then cook it over a steady flow of steam for about 30 minutes (see page 98).

tamarind

Crescent-shaped pods of tamarind fruit dangle from huge hardwood trees throughout Southeast Asia. Tamarind liquid is made by soaking ripe tamarind pulp and pressing it through a strainer to create a thick, luscious purée that is earthy brown, smoky, sour, and sweet (see page 150). Taste it right away, noting its flavor. Then you can stir in sugar to balance a batch after a few days, since it sharpens with time. I keep a batch covered and refrigerated for up to a week. Its color enhances *paht Thai* (page 107), among other dishes. Thai cooks routinely use plain white vinegar or freshly squeezed lime juice in place of tamarind liquid. Other good substitutes are Indian-style tamarind chutney, or a mix of equal parts of white vinegar, sugar, and soy sauce.

tapioca flour

Look for this delicate bright white flour in small, well-labeled plastic or paper packets, sold alongside rice flour in Asian markets. Valued for its many uses in preparing traditional sweets and snacks, it combines with rice flour to form the noodle-like pancake in Crispy Omelet with Oysters and Bean Sprouts (page 60). You can use a combination of equal parts all-purpose flour and cornstarch in place of rice flour and tapioca flour if need be.

turmeric

This knobby cousin of ginger and galanga, known as *khamin* in Thai and *nghe* in Vietnamese, is beloved not for its flavor, which is quite mild, but for its outrageous pumpkin orange hue, which it transmits vigorously to food and everything else it touches. It has been prized for centuries as a dye for cloth, most notably for the traditional robes of Theravada Buddhist monks. You may find whole rhizomes of turmeric fresh or frozen in Asian markets. I have used ground dried turmeric in these recipes because it is so easy to find and use, and because it does a beautiful job of transmitting its gorgeous hue. To use fresh or frozen turmeric, peel and mince it; or chop coarsely and then mash it to a paste with a mortar and pestle; or grind it to a paste with some of the liquid ingredients in a given recipe. Expect its color on anything it touches. On your hands and cutting board it wears off quickly, but on cloth it is permanent.

wild lime leaves

These sturdy, smooth, and shiny leaves from the wild lime tree impart Thai soups and curries with a spectacular burst of intense, exotic citrus flavor and perfume. Called *daun limau perut* in Malaysia, wild lime leaves are sometimes referred to with the word "kaffir," a deeply offensive term used as a racial slur. I gladly leave that archaic usage behind, since "wild" is botanically descriptive, already in common usage, and easy to remember and spell. Wild lime leaves grow in pairs on the extremely thorny emerald green *mah-krood* tree, a tropical native that can be small enough to fit in a 2-gallon pot, and yet grow tall enough to shade a college basketball team. You will find wild lime leaves in small sacks and on shrink-wrapped trays in Asian markets. If you do not see any fresh ones, ask if they carry frozen wild lime leaves. Dried lime leaves are simply useless, just like dried lemongrass, but do not despair: In any recipe in this book you can omit them and still have a wonderful and delicious Thai dish. Fresh wild lime leaves freeze very well, so if you encounter a supply only occasionally, buy lots of them and divide all the leaves among small resealable plastic bags. Keep one of these small bags handy on the freezer shelf to use as your daily supply, and combine the remaining small sealed bags of lime leaves into one large resealable plastic bag. Seal it up tightly and place it deep in the freezer until you need more wild lime leaves. Use frozen wild lime leaves straight from the freezer, without thawing.

MAIL-ORDER SOURCES FOR THAI INGREDIENTS

Adriana's Caravan
409 Vanderbilt Street
Brooklyn, NY 11218
(800) 316-0820
Fax: (718) 436-8565
www.adrianascaravan.com

Import Food Thai Supermarket
P.O. Box 2054
Issaquah, WA 98027
(425) 392-7516
Fax: (425) 392-7516
www.importfood.com

Kalustyan's
123 Lexington Avenue
New York, NY 10016
(212) 685-3451
Fax: (212) 683-8458
www.kalustyans.com

Temple of Thai
P.O. Box 112
Carroll, IA 51401
(877) 811-8773
Fax: (712) 792-0698
www.templeofthai.com

INDEX

table of equivalents

The exact equivalents in the following tables have been rounded for convenience.

Liquid/Dry Measures

U.S.	Metric
¼ teaspoon	1.25 milliliters
½ teaspoon	2.5 milliliters
1 teaspoon	5 milliliters
1 tablespoon (3 teaspoons)	15 milliliters
1 fluid ounce (2 tablespoons)	30 milliliters
¼ cup	60 milliliters
⅓ cup	80 milliliters
½ cup	120 milliliters
1 cup	240 milliliters
1 pint (2 cups)	480 milliliters
1 quart (4 cups, 32 ounces)	960 milliliters
1 gallon (4 quarts)	3.84 liters
1 ounce (by weight)	28 grams
1 pound	454 grams
2.2 pounds	1 kilogram

Length

U.S.	Metric
⅛ inch	3 millimeters
¼ inch	6 millimeters
½ inch	12 millimeters
1 inch	2.5 centimeters

Oven Temperature

Fahrenheit	Celsius	Gas
250	120	½
275	140	1
300	150	2
325	160	3
350	180	4
375	190	5
400	200	6
425	220	7
450	230	8
475	240	9
500	260	10